THE LONG WAY HOME

The Best of the LITTLE RED BOOK Series

1998-2008

Edited by RD Armstrong

ISBN 978-1-929878-04-8

First edition

Lummox Press
PO Box 5301
San Pedro, CA 90733

www.lummoxpress.com

The Lummox Press wishes to thank the estates of Philomene Long and
John Thomas for permission to publish their poems, as well as, the editors
of any magazines that these poems may have appeared in.

Introduction

By RD Armstrong

When I first conceived of the idea for the Little Red Book series (or LRB), I had just published two small books with very distinctive fire engine red covers (these later became LRB 1 & 2). The second book was a short story entitled El Pagano and was written in what I thought was a gritty, noir / pulp style. Eventually I would republish it as the centerpiece for a collection of short stories of my own. But in the humble beginnings of the Lummox Press, the LRB would become a series that poets would eventually seek out to be included in.

An English Prof at a local university suggested to me that if I wanted the Lummox Press to be taken seriously, I'd better start publishing other poets, lest I become known as a Vanity Press, an ignoble fate to be sure. Had I known better I might have opted for the Vanity Press status – at least I would be getting paid for the books I published; unlike the losing proposition that most Small or Alternative Small Presses suffer from – this "labor of love" mentality. It's a fine line between enjoying a modicum of success and failing with panache.

In the world of small press poetry, the truly pure poet is a voice for the muse and isn't concerned with such mundane tasks as the cost of production or sales or promotion (that's somebody else's job). As long as he or she is getting the accolades of the crowd (plus a little folding green), that's enough. Unfortunately, while the maker of the poems doesn't have to do anything else to demonstrate their genius, the maker of the book (the vehicle by which their genius is presented to the world) has to try every conceivable method to bring the world to them. Otherwise, what's the point of doing the book in the first place? Oh yeah, that "labor of love" thing.

And here in lies the rub. Publishing, whether it's on a mammoth or miniscule scale is work. Sometimes it's hard work, sometimes not. But even if it's a part-time job, it gets old fast when you're not getting compensated for your time. It doesn't have to be money, there are other ways to be compensated. Granted, money talks loud and clear, but it also comes and goes mighty fast. The other forms of compensation that last are things like friendship. To be successful in an operation like the Lummox Press, in other words, to keep the flame alive, one has to develop a partnership with those you are publishing. This is probably also true for the larger presses and publishing houses. The writer of the poetry has to be willing to get out there and promote the book. If that doesn't happen, if they don't take an active role in promoting their own work, then the enterprise is doomed from the get-go.

As you might guess I'm speaking from experience. I never planned on doing this series for ten years. I never thought I'd be publishing so many widely divergent voices from the small press poetry world, either; nor did I know that I would make so many friends/enemies doing this. I just did it.

So, on the tenth anniversary of the Little Red Book series, I decided it was time to publish a sampling of some of the best poems, with a few exceptions. LRB 2 is a story that can be found in El Pagano and Other Twisted tales (www.lummoxpress.com) and LRB 11 was a sampler and so, a redundancy. A few other titles are not represented because of falling outs between publisher and poet. It is my hope that upon reading these poems, you, the reader, will want to delve further into this series and purchase some of these Little Red Books for yourself. Almost all of the titles are available through the Lummox press website for the paltry sum of $6 (US) and $8 (World) each.

Enjoy.

Two from FOOL'S PARADISE #1

The Hell I Made in Your Honor

Here's to the dull thud that
the "other" shoe makes
when it hits home at last.
When it dawns on you
what's really going down
and you see that the
bed you've made
in the devil's mouth
is beginning to teeter,
is it destiny (again)
or oblivion that calls
you by your secret name?

On The Margin

A loose mirror on the passenger side
A leaky seal
King-pins that need replacing
A failing wheel cylinder
A broken camera lens
Bad tubes
Dull blades
Unpaid debts
Broken dreams
No hot water in the bathroom

Stains on the sheets
Dirty smudges on the walls
A weed choked garden
A hair-choked drain
A few steps from insanity
A few more steps from a cardboard box under a bridge
One step from an early grave
A strange hand in your pocket
A finger on the trigger
A pain in the ass
Blood in the toilet
A bald tire – a wet, oily street
The wrong time to turn over a new leaf
A broken rubber
A broken heart
An insensitive remark
A caution thrown to the wind
 Boredom
Four walls closing in fast

It's not the big issues that take you out
It's the little moments that ambush you –
A broken pencil
Or your computer crashing with all your poetry
Erased

RD Armstrong

Two from EQUAL OPPORTUNITY SLEDGEHAMMER #3

Scarecrow

Sherrise Iverson and Matthew Shepard
hand me the songbooks of love.
Get the words right when you roar out loud
I wanted to find the right kind of food
to match the hope fighting to stay alive
inside the hunger. Turn to your right,
dream a little left. The city on the hill
is made of mud. The city on the hill won't know your name
unless you belt it out
with all your pain, empathy, and belief.
The antihomosexual gang outside Matthew Shepard's
funeral this afternoon waved signs that
said He Is Going To Hell.
Hell, though, being right here on Earth,
was not filled with anyone but them.
Hell, being right here, is the residence Jeffrey
Strohmeier lives in when he tells me over my TV imagery
that everyone is to blame for Sherrise but him.
A lot of people were able to fit in that
Stateline women's bathroom according to such a theory.
Match that hope trying to stay alive in your hunger.
Listen to the bruised airline of burning
it crashes repeatedly in the name of hate
and hate's natural father and mother, fear.
The poor biker who discovered Shepard in a coma
tied to a fence said he looked at first like a Scarecrow
and scarecrows are easy to burn down into amnesia
and hate's natural mother and father want you to donate
money and time to the future
the orchestra of fist, the aria of bludgeon, the rhythm
and blues of strangulation, ah, the air is opening
to allow the air to enter, the air is thinning out now, just
like the crowd, and alone
we stumble up the trail toward the welcome home of hope.
Shepard beaten so hard they could see brain stem
subzero dancehall of large quiet sky
much larger than the claustrophobic end game
Strohmeier gave Sherrise
can the bag of empathy hold?

can the game be called on account of dark?
Scarecrows are easy to tear apart in this resumé of
crow
less
faith
Those antihomosexual folks at Shepard's funeral
called him a Sodomite and because of that he deserved
a life in Hell, whatever Hell other than this one
at times could be
Those antihomosexual folks with their predictable one note
rage
have committed a much darker offense
They haven't fucked anyone in the ass
but they have fucked all believers of empathy and tolerance
in the heart
and as you know from your medical journals
a hole in the heart is a hard one to come in out
of the rain from
It snowed in casper this afternoon
as Matthew Shepard got placed
his two killers, both young, await their dance card in jail
rumors abound that one of them has already said
he deserves to die
Strohmeier in Nevada told me David Cash his pal was a bad man
and a horrible human
David Cash is currently enrolled in Berkeley
getting a degree in something certainly not Feeling
The federal government sent down one of their "gay"
representatives to the funeral in Casper
One hell of a job description, that, "gay" representative
Turn around now. Grab the one you love. Grab yourself
if you don't love anyone.
Turn around now and show me how you can move to the unheard
music. Turn around
and show me the shape of the country you live in, and through.
Sing one for Sherrise Iverson
Sing one for Matthew Shepard
Sing one for Jeffrey Strohmeier who just realized his friend
David Cash was not a good friend
Sing one for david Cash who may run into himself one day but I doubt it
Sing one for those two guys in Wyoming who tore Matthew
Shepard apart for no reason
You never need a reason to show how easy you can tear something apart
Sing one for me
Sing one for you
Keep singing when the lights go down
We'll make a record

It'll be swell
We'll make a damn fine record
Sing one for Sherrise Iverson's daddy
who was too busy gambling
to make sure she was okay
Casinos are made, of course, for little children
Sing one for those antihomosexual assholes
who just had to come to shepard's funeral
to send him off in their own empathetic style
They fuck my heart still
They fuck my heart so bad I can't ever ask them back
We all make such a damn fine sound
Sherries Iverson and Matthew Shepard give us our sheet music
Sing my friend and
sing like you've never sung one before
You got a damn wonderful voice

10/16/98

bucketful of yes

   hold the earth in your hand today
   the circus is moving into your bedroom
   all the animals are gold
   the government finally on hiatus
   not likely to return for years
   when the armies implode
   no war tonight on the dinner table
   excited hair murmurs of wind
   sleep easy guarding the door
   nobody irritable is due soon
    hold your own in the ongoing investigation
    tap your favorite tune with your toes
    they'll be coming around soon enough
     with gossip and drugs to ease the pain
      it won't be for some time though
and the dancefloor has just opened up a bank account in your heart
  no dying needed tonight on the table
    all the animals let you into their cages
     they recognize the school you came out of
      they love the cut of your soul

5/10/98
Scott Wannberg

Four from BONE #4

willie had a

stutter & his big
brother carl always
did his talking for
him except when their
father died the old
man had been an alkie
& the only people
who went to the
funeral were his old
drinking pals even
the minister shor
tened the prayer &
got out quick &
while the wind was
blowing up a blue
norther willie got
his bugle out of
the car it was
covered w/dings &
scratches & had a
whoop ass sticker
slapped on the
brass but when
willie started to
play taps none of
that mattered it
was a low down
gravelly version of
the piece & when
he finished the
song went up into
the storm & stayed
sweet in the rain

after

the reading
this guy came
up to me sd
you write
good but
that's not a
poem he was
shaking a
glass full
of bourbon
laced w/ice
right then
i didn't
give a fuck
what he
thought
because the
lines were
still riding
down my bones
so i went
into a low
crouch like
i was abt
to fire a
right cross &
when he tried
to duck away
i sd if it
kicks yr ass
pal it's a
poem

Todd Moore

Tank Farm

Lou was welding
on top of the tank
when a spark ignited
a ghost vapor
and blew him
clean in half.
I couldn't stop
shakin' for a week
so the company sent
me to Port Angeles.
Beneath the Olympic
Glaciers I finally
slept easy and
the coffee began to
taste good again.

The Road (More or Less Traveled)

Day's end and I'm
picking up pieces
of past lives
scattered across this plane
of memory.
It is an incomplete geometry
with angles so obtuse
they will not intersect,
the whys outnumber the ex's
and yet, they still add up to zero.
Day's end and I'm
unsure what the product is.
These calculations
should add up to sum-thing
but I'm not sure what its value is.
The road winds on ahead
of me, and even though I left
the station at four thirty and
have been traveling at sixty
miles per hour, I still don't
know when I will arrive

or, worse yet, where.

RD Armstrong

One from MEAT EATER #5

Dialogue again & again

I don't need a goddamn soul, I hollered. Not ONE GODDAMN PERSON. Not now, not ever.

World, I added, you are a stone mother-fucker.

Two hours ago I had shot up a speedball, felt my heart leave a chest, & an hour later, come back. I was feeling cocky, heroin & speed clearing the MeKong Delta sludge from my eyes.

Kill me, I said to the ghosts, come on kill me. It's you or the fucking heroin – either way, I'm going to die.

Not a one showed their mutilated head.

What'd you do – leave with that woman? I screamed my questions t the walls. I don't need a gun to kill you anymore, I'll run into Hell with you.

An hour to a hit; I was planning my days around withdrawals. An overdose was laughed at.

I fell asleep with a Purple Heart on my lap.

Bill Shields

Two from SCAR TISSUE #6

POEM FOR FATHER

I found my father's old Kodak camera
While cleaning the house on summer
My brother says that it's an antique
That he saw one just like it
In a museum in Los Angeles
Click
        Click
                Click

Flash back past/present
No future
1940 girl in nylons
And hard thighs
With seams up to paradise
Right there in the palm of my hands

Sears Roebuck catalog store model
Jumps back in like a keystone camera
The mystery of life
Click
        Click
                Click

Mother's smiling face

Click
        Click
                Click

Lens opens/shuts
Records what might have been
Could have been
Should have been
The steel cold
To the touch

SAYING GOODBYE

Death travels a lonely road
Creeping up to you like
A mugger
A black crow poised
In its nest
Waiting for the human soul
To be laid to rest
Neither words or stones
Detract it from its mission

I see you laid out
For viewing
Given over to
The undertaker's art

The family rarely together
Paying their last respects
Lady death casting her net
Across a river
Of invisible tears

A.D. Winans

Two from APOLOGY TO THE IDIOTS #7

naked brunch w/ pencils & minds unlike us

my cat wants to sleep by himself. But I don't.
Pencils are good because you know they never run out
of ink just space.
There's a strange man living in my basement
for the past 15yrs. & he's a nice man. I think.
Very little controls my stomach which my brain adores.
Pot can only be introduced to a moderately happy setting/
nerves put all bliss or tolerable things off for worse
parties of the mind.
Pencil points may break
but also maintain good probability of resolution.
It gets worse when you start believing in psychology
or anything that isn't believing in nothing
nothing is a lonely good thing
it's unresponsive when all responses are bad.
I hate shitting
maybe it was a bad experience
up the ass
when I was a kid
because all the haunting things happen when yr' a kid
just never delivered until yr' not ready for it.
The more I know the more it sucks
because what I know
sucks.
Poems used to save me.
Poetry is a bad habit. To fuck. I mean kick.
Now put the two together.
Don't kick anything
just be nice to it & maybe it'll walk away
because s/x s/things walk when you're not waiting.
Try to close yr' eyes again & play fetus & hope
it goes far enough away to write to it/
send it yr' love/
hope it gets lost
in the mail/
in the mind

I AM a woman

maybe
i'll cut these tits off
stand on totem/
pretend it's penis
& scream
w/ ears closed
to animals/
screaming s/thing feminine
w/ spinning boob guts.
RAW/
angry
on totem
because ground
too timid/ often
too loud.
Scream s/thing more feminine than
vagina
words that still write
when vexating voices
have ran off w/
relaxed
pretty
ears

Laura Joy Lustig

Eight from EYES LIKE MINGUS #8

the saxophone is next to the pepper

after
trying everything
       from
classical to rap,
it seems I cook
better to jazz.
Jazz brings out the
taste. It must be
the way I cook. If
a recipe is a melody,
I won't necessarily keep
the same order of notes.
You add a dash here
and take away a pinch
there. Leave it to your
wrists – let your tongue
be the judge. And when
it works, you get that
rainbow in your mouth
instead of your ears.

Robert Underwood

Poem For CHARLIE PARKER

he played the nerve ends
like a skilled violinist
losing himself
in sightless sound
playing deep down
from the gut
all the way
to the balls

he played as if death
was playing tag

with his shadow
each note bathed in blood
leaving you with that
chalk scraping against blackboard
gut wrenching chill

AD Winans

BUD POWELL

the bandstand is bouncing
human confusion
blurred
into palpable resolution
we are filled
with a thousand ghosts
stepping right out of our shoes
while fetching that shiny thing
bang those 88s
to hell and back
tell them heaven
isn't slippers
shuffling down
an endless well lit hallway
but dancing on red hot coals
jumping higher
.....higher

Mark Hartenbach

PLAYING THE CHANGES

I asked Horace
if he wanted some coffee
he said, "Bean?"
I said, "Yeah, what other kind is there?"
he said, "Instant, freeze-dried, decaf."

Same thing
when I asked him how he liked

our steinway grand
at the Outpost, our jazz club
he said, "Yeah," thoughtful pauses
between words, "Wood, you know," drag
on his cigarette, "It's authentic."

Mark Weber— 12june98

kerouac on the

radio it's an
old show taped back in the
60's maybe a
sax in the back
ground & Jack's
talking abt
some bar he
used to go in
to & suddenly
i'm not driving
down central
anymore i'm
right there in
the bar & some
body buys a
round jack
tells abt the
way he gets
poems it's
like tapping
a cigaret out
of a pack
& you know
what he sez
dropping a
dime in the
bar water
they taste
like nictine
& beer

Todd Moore

The Power, He Has The Power

When Benny Russell rode a soprano sax
                across the East river
scaling Manhattan's sky
                                back
into an open mouthed crowd
before they knew what took
                                their breath

knew he had it:

                        not Empire State
                                Twin Towers
                                Wall Street's

sound reverberated

                        His. . .

Turned loose a woman
vamped & moaned & came
in nearly dark, stage lit promenade,
limp against the rail:
                Heart beating drums . . . bass
                                Now
grabbed a tenor sax
and went berserk: jumped,
stamped his feet, motorcycling
off notes, roared up & down
                                buildings . . .

soprano sax
                screaming
                                higher

                        higher

                woman/man
                naked   shameless
                        one

Linda Lerner

ella

ella fitzgerald sang
oxygen got discovered
the sun, on its way to the bank to make a deposit
just sort of had to hang there a minute
bopping down and up to the tune
of ella's singing
ella fitzgerald sang
cities rose up from the dirt
the buildings of them had people
inside them and
inside those people there were
stories and bloodstreams
that were the songs ella
fitzgerald sang
the sun really had to make it to the bank
before it closed
otherwise it would be overdrawn
and when the sun gets overdrawn
we get burned
ella fitzgerald sang
armies threw down their guns
the time for dying
had not come to just yet
the sun hovered there
not wanting to go
ella fitzgerald sang
and the stories in her songs
are the stories that keep
us from going under

Scott Wannberg— 6-18-96

Eyes   Like Mingus
(For Steve Fowler)

Eyes   like flint
         like flecks of coal
         like shiny bits of starless sky
         trapped in the ruins of a slag heap

Eyes   like molten steel
         sullen and angry

piercing -- a bullet finding its mark
like a jaguar
passionate and alive
yet hating the trap
pacing behind the bars
bars like a skeleton
trapped inside the mind
behind

Eyes   like Mingus
like notes caught in the net
like the grid of notation
like Mingus
in shamanic Mexico
trapped in a chair
no strength to grip
no fingers to coax notes with
no feet to stand up and count with
no time -- no signature

Eyes   like concrete -- shattering
like glass -- splintering
like the wrecking ball's slap
like voltage -- unregulated
like a passion laid bare
to the gallery's scrutiny
like the madman's frothing nightmare
like the inexplicable accuracy of random fate
like a shot to the gut
like Coltrane's "Favorite Things"
like your fingers -- stilled

Eyes   like an empty glass
staring bug-eyed into space
upturned and dispassionate
like a dream -- lost in the stars

Eyes   like Mingus
silent but never
silenced.

RD Armstrong

Two from REMEMBERING BUKOWSKI #9

WAITING FOR THE BIG SCORE

Sixteen years high
On this hill
On Laidley street
Writing these words
Drinking the hard stuff
Playing the horses
Waiting on the big score
And sometimes it's steak
And eggs
But most of the time
It's hamburger helper
And noodles
Waiting for the exacta
To come in
At Golden Gate Fields
Waiting on the big score
Waiting on the American dream
And after another day of losing
It's back to North Beach
Sitting at Gino and Carlo's bar
Eyeing the daily scratch sheet
Looking at the early morning line
Feeling like Bukowski
Must have felt
Keeping an eye out
For the poets
Who line-up
Like a bad daily double
At Bay Meadows
My eyes scanning
The scratch sheet
Looking for the big kill
Silky Sullivan
16 lengths back
Making his move down
The backstretch

All those sad faces coming
To life
Moving briskly toward
The winner's circle
A matinee idols dream
Come true

My life on the line
Like a long row of hot
Dogs moving down
That long line
At the butcher factory
Waiting on the big score
The crowd yelling wildly
Silky Sullivan racing across
The finish line
Winner by a nose

The tote board lighting up
Like a Christmas tree
And then the announcer says
LADIES AND GENTLEMEN
Please hold on to your tickets
An official inquiry has been made
And then it's official
A disqualification
For bumping in the stretch
Silky Sullivan is moved
From first to last
Hypnotic Agent is second
Perverse Fantasy is declared
The winner
And it's back
To Gino and Carlo's bar
The big score
No more
Left feeling
Like a man going
To bed with Madonna
And waking up
In the morning
Next to Barbara
Bush

FEELING LIKE HANK DID AT AGE 61

Tossing and turning
In bed
Unable to sleep
And when I do
The night sweats and dreams
Tear at my soul
Approaching sixty
With an arthritic neck
A moustache turned gray
While women look
The other way
Each year the poems
Come harder leaving
Me feeling like a lifer
Marking time
My body dodging life's cruel
Blows
Feeling like a boxer asked
To take a dive
Being beaten up on
Knocked down
Getting up each time
Beating the count
Knowing you can't win
Can't beat the odds
Lady death panting down
The back of your neck
Refusing to throw in
The towel
Nose bleeding
Head pounding
Jabbing punching going
The full ten rounds
Hoping to get something
Better than a draw

A.D. Winans

Excerpt from A JOURNEY UP THE COAST #10

Driving up 101
found myself drifting
into the memory lane on
more than one
occasion.
Many treks up and
down this highway --
this stretch of road
in the fine company
of the comrades of
youth --
friends and lovers
companions of those daze
so many years / miles ago
and now I fly solo
(so low).
Funny how certain landscape
features trigger certain
memories
like dreams re-activated
by the piano roll of
time
the
subconscious mind tips open
the dusty old photo album
and out tumbles pictures
from another time --
Karen and her '58 Chevy
four door   bruising tank of a car
riding north through Paso Robles
in the heat of that summer
101 a two-lane country road
in those days   Karen long gone
now.
Thought of her much
this first time on 101
in a dozen years easy.
Look forward to the sad dumb beauty of

these memories as trip unfolds
after house uncurls itself and
the coffee pot is empty.

ROUTE ONE

Two lanes winding
out of desolate coast
lined with sheer cliffs
flat gray drops
into sheetmetal patina sea
cliffs topped with scrub
and bush and wild grasses
wildly rioting at roadside
or freshly mowed and baled
like a KS wheatfield.
Little towns of Davenport
Pescadero, Half Moon
Maltera and Venice Beach
"Where's the sunglasses?"
Even San Pedro (park)
"Am I going south or north?"
Pass a gutted and wind-blasted
concrete shell of a house --
it has no access
no explanation
just stands on the
weathered pedestal of sandstone
perched on top of a hill
over-looking Half Moon Bay.
This stretch
winding
up to the outskirts
of SanFran's suburbs
leads a caravan
away from the isolation
of the rugged coastline
and into Daly City's "little
boxes" made of ticky-tack
once a novelty
now the common
denominator.

RD Armstrong

Two from THE INSIDE OUT WORLD OF B.Z. NIDITCH #12

Ecology Study

You had to dash off
somewhere by the river
in the muggy August
to find samples of stones.
I said, trekking up Beacon Hill,
"The hell with that today!
Stay with me.
Put on some Nina Simone
and wait, you're forgetting
your jacket anyway."

But you went alone
to the Charles River
under scrambled clouds
raining from a hungry heaven
and then you coming back
in tatters, unbuttoning yourself,
still prejudiced
toward your experiment,
but grateful for my angst.

Two in August

To the mountain's western face
a full sun appears
to light crannies of the sky
advancing the day
butterflies and roses emerge
sunshine flecks by the breeze
near the cliffs
buffeted by feathery winds
passing two in a car
ousted by the city
unbuckled and propped up
to watch nature's border country
crossing uncharted roads
magnifying shrubs and flora
passing unnamed mapled suburbs
where greensward shadows
hide a maze of fauna
near the hot rocks
which glittered in the sands
by the slow traffic
on a makeshift holiday
by miles of field-stone.

B.Z. Niditch

Two from HANG GLIDING ON X #13

Funk Out

Parliament Funkadelic
made me decide not to
kill myself. Planned on
slitting my wrists; had
the note prepared; cat
squared away for a few
days at least. But
for some reason
instead of listening to
my standard
goth death metal
I was listening to funk
-- kool ole shit --
when I heard we've got to
"tear the roof off the sucker --
(give up the funk)" -- and for
some unknown reason,
I started grooving and put
some Meat beat Manifesto
on and then some
Renegade Soundwave
and I was off, grooving.
The
cat must have thought
I was nuts.

He wasn't too far off.

Time to Fly

there are things inside you
and me

      atrocities

waiting to be committed
like my shoving this knife
into you
      or me
and we love and hate
with equal madness

let's kill each other

please

Scott Holstad

Four from ANY ABYSS WILL DO #14

Hotel #1

A hotel room somewhere
in a town you're glad you never
lived in
two people
in bed drinking beer and wine
smoking cigarettes
she telling him about the time
when she was 14
one of her father's
friends tied her to a
chair and raped her and
when he was done he told her
he would kill her if she ever
told anybody
she believed him and so she
never did
until now
he only half
listening watching the smoke
drift about the room
not knowing what to say just
wanting her to stop
crying
telling her
it's okay pouring her another
glass of wine wondering
when she would be drunk enough
to let him fuck her.

Poems Like Bloody Teeth

It's been years since I last
saw you

and still you manage
to pull poems from me like bloody
teeth

somewhere you are smiling
because you always told me
this is how
it would be

I too am smiling
because I always knew
you were right.

Some Truths

They say you're nothing
but a
self
serving
manipulative
unattractive
whore
with dumb
face
crooked
mouth
&
heart of
cardboard.

I say your drunken
laughter at
3 a.m.
is more beautiful
than god.

They are right

and I am right.

I buy you another drink with the
understanding

that some truths
matter more

than others.

The World

The world is not much.
If you've got nothing better
to do
say
on a sunday
afternoon
you can watch
how easily it
comes apart
in your hands
breaks into
sharp and ugly
little
pieces
and
if you're still bored you can
pick one up and
carve a message to yourself
deep
beneath the skin
wait a bit and see
if you still remember
how to
bleed.

Will Taylor Jr.

Three from BLOOD ON THE FLOOR #15

throwing tears at the stones   3/22/99

the last thing she remembered was
the jewish girls being led barefoot
through the snow & into the gas
chambers singing hatikvah.

these days
she knows the arabs passion
as she watches silently their
eyes peering over the timeless
devil hair of barbed wire.
these days
it is her ritual to walk the
long robes of steel & pass
roses across the miles
of tangled differences

& it is her custom
to consider this piece of
space flesh called earth
in terms of iron & flowers- -
in terms of songs that
can not be heard - -
in terms of the silences
that are too loud
for anyone to bare.

everything butchers everything - -

the arabs butcher the jews
the jews butcher the arabs
her sister in america butchers
the hours with soap opera
all systems butcher passion

it is all much of the same.
the differences in stone
that neither time nor technology
can reverse.

she bows before the wailing wall.
she speaks to the old ghosts as
if they are the unborn children
of tomorrow - -

these days to the passing observer
it would appear she is just
another old woman in black
with nothing more to do

but throw tears at the stones

blood on the floor   **2/28/99**

don't slip
there is blood on the floor.

blood of apathy
blood of the dispassionate
the ignoring
blood of those numbed by dumb
life
blood of those who pretend it
never happens / the cheerfully
humbled who go about it all
smiling.

blood of the corpses that have
not yet died
the baby 15 yrs into life
not yet born
the ancient one bereft of wisdom
not yet lived.

blood of the holy filthy
blood on the godhead
blood of the rich in their
diamond fishbowls
the paparazzi in their glory
the machines in their monopoly
the innocent in their strangulation
the earth in her silence.

don't slip
the anomalies are pure
the sky is red
the raindrops are loaded
with the eyes of children

don't slip
there is blood on the floor.

homesickness without an address

in this sordid wilderness
under all this mess
it is homesickness keeps us alive

we go because to stay is not
we arrive because we have not found

we move through the mist of indifference
we are egged on by notions of a 4th dimension

we are lost in the theaters
humored amongst the metaphors
ignored in the language of machines & tigers

there is no song of songs, just noise
there is no silence, just sound

it is homesickness without an address
homesickness that urges us on

to be still is to merge with the mire
to move is to be possible

we survive because we are lost
we arrive because we are going

normal

Three from MAYTAG HEIGHTS #16

STREET POET

he walks the streets
bent over
looking like an old man
with eyes empty
as a broken parking meter
weighed down by the years
his mind heavy as an anchor
dragging the ocean floor
beaten-down rebel
playing old Lorca ballads
in his heart
his mind destroyed
by shock treatments
and one too many doses
of police nightsticks
at night he dreams
he is riding with geronimo
has imaginary conversations
with Charlie Parker
rides the ferry
with Coltrane and Mingus
getting off at Bourbon Street
tp share a drink with Kerouac
shares a cigarette
with Charlie Chaplin
at the old Bijou theater
rides the subway with Bob Kaufman
getting off at 56th street
forever
walks the battlefields
with Walt Whitman
rides the plains
with Red Cloud

in search of the last buffalo
walking the streets of north beach
in search of the elusive
ginger fish smell
his dreams of america
destroyed by assassinations
and conspiracies
old red white and blue
replaced by discarded newspapers
to fend off the cold

A.D. Winans

THE MAN AT MY WINDOW

Sitting in our old truck,
a man comes up to the window
and asks for spare change.

My young daughter looks appalled,
wondering why he needs money,
and suddenly I remember

when it was the two of us
living out of this old truck.
But she was only twelve weeks old,
too young to remember. Only six years
have passed since we lived in this truck,
yet, while looking for spare change.

I remember how slowly those weeks passed
as we drove down the road listening
to lullabies and children tapes at night,

pretending everything was all right,
though I had no idea where we'd sleep.
After eight months, we finally moved

into a home, and friends said those homeless months
would leave my daughter permanently scarred,
which I refused to believe because I was conjuring

up images of nomadic people while
feeling my daughter's endless nursing.
And years later, I'm digging up change,

touching hands with another kindred spirit.

Diane Payne

The Scars on Your Back Sing

i'm a zealot in
the year of
hunger strikes

water
once a day in
a room with a desk
and a typewriter

my body designed
to reject god
as violently as
possible
but
you grow bored with

this line of
thought

the scars
on your back sing
songs
you forgot they knew

and to be
relatively healthy
and talk of pain
is to
risk offending
the truly broken

it's
a simple fact
not a show of
concern

and again
you turn away

your silence more
holy
than my words

my hands with
the teeth of
mad dogs

both of us
positive
we own the truth

John Sweet

Two from ME #17

Me

Cystitis and the doctor
tells me "Don't do anything
sexually until this is cleared
up," but everything is sexual,
bra, nipples, breasts, even under
my stretch nylon dress, my legs
alive with pantyhose, heels,
makeup, eyes, hair, everything
says touch, explore, play, ME,
ME, ME expelled from the Eden
of my own body.

For Those I Leave Behind

Zen into the core
of every moment,
moment by moment,
hour by, year by
decade,
NOW
NOW
NOW,
I see Amazonas
water lily pads,
huge, water buffalos
and a naked black African
girl, the Urubamba River,
vultures eating
fish-guts, wharves at Belém,
my wife's face going from 20
to 80 in as long as it takes
to write these
lines.

Hugh/Connie Fox

Three from THE ICEBERG THEORY #18

I Like Cats that Catch Things

i never discourage a cat's natural instinct
to catch things.

i love it when a cat catches a rat. who wouldn't?
our cats probably spare us many plagues. we
have three cats in our house and it is not a
popular getaway-weekend for rats.

i don't even mind it when a cat catches a bird.
there seem to be many species of birds that are
not endangered. generally a cat will bite right

through the top of a bird's skull and puncture its
brain. it ain't pretty, but it's effective. and,
after all, since birds can fly and cats can't,
it's quite an accomplishment for a cat to catch
a bird, even though many birds, pigeons in
particular, can be mighty stupid. i would
never discourage a cat from catching even the
most beautiful of birds (excluding the kids'
parakeet). birds are a cat's proudest trophies,
like santiago's big fish was his.

i just wish they wouldn't insist on bringing
all the bloody, furry, feathery fuckers into
the house for our dinner guests to admire.

Gimme a Break

at sim's coffee shop on the corner
of bellflower boulevard and spring street,
across from the enormous cal worthington
ford dealership, i order the club sandwich

and sit observing its layers of turkey,

bacon, tomatoes and lettuce on double-
decker toasted white bread. i remove
the toothpick from one triangle, sink

my teeth into it, lick the rich ling-
ering mayonnaise from my mustache. this
sandwich will cost me a little over four
dollars. it includes potato salad, half

a pickle, a slice of carrot. i could not
buy this sandwich in london if i had
just held up the bank of england. i doubt
that i could duplicate it in paris.

so please don't mention nitrites,
cholesterol, pesticides, or the lack of
fiber. let me just savor what any child could
tell us: how wonderful an American sandwich

tastes. and if you do fuck up this lunch for
me, i swear i'll eat nothing but cheeseburgers
and tuna sandwiches until there's not a dolphin
left in what used to be the rainforests.

the days go awry

it's a beautiful southern california day:
eighty-six degrees in january and i'm swimming
at the heated outdoor pool of the local ymca,
gazing up from my sidestroke,
like a giant sea otter
(even sporting the whiskers)
at the perfectly blue skies
and the deep green pine trees
etched against them,

and the combination of weather, aesthetics,
and endorphins puts me in such a benevolent
mood that i want to do more nice things for
her, go places with her, have romantic
outings again,
but then i realize that at this very moment
she is probably in a vile temper and
blaming it on precisely this early summer,
as her allergies flare up,
and her students grow unruly,

and i remember what bukowski used to write me
about women--how he'd wake up to a new day
in a generally positive frame of mind--
and yes that's possible even when hungover--
and then he'd notice that whatever woman he was
with was sitting there, silent, stewing, just
waiting to ruin it all,
and he couldn't figure it out about women,
what it was about women that impelled them
towards unhappiness--i suppose today we'd
just say "hormones"--and as i contemplated how
often she has brought me down,
with her complaints and complications,
my heart begins to sink,

and i sneeze.

Gerald Locklin

Three from NO EARTHLY SENSE
GETS IT RIGHT #19

This Was the Year

Love yanked me up
from my father's death;
this year I shelved my hatred
like ancestral linen
and gave up mourning
a father I never had.

I sprang out of my head
into zombie haunted streets,
dodging computerized lives,
irrelevant bodies,
a year a man and I spent
tasting each other with our eyes,
tonguing words.

Vendors shouted ice cream and hot dogs
down my ears, Koreans gorged me
with fresh anything;
I let the sun go mad
as a rabid dog on my fair skin,
and not once heard
my mother's warning voice.
I reached out to love
with more imagination, more woman
than someone knew what to do with,
the year
the present moment is fast ripening
in this first June sun.

Halloween 1997

the dead wake from poems
i've buried them in
calling long distance
                    how far from dementia
i don't ask   a mother
calling her teen age runaway
                         not me...

risen from the kaddish
my father hit me with
for disobedience: nobody's child/

i've earned the right:

wasn't me she bathed fed
clothed sent to school
even knew
                                    but sounds ok...
if i had a daughter/don't
but if i did
i'd want one like her
as wild & bad
locked up with that lover
my mother imagines me with
not stuck in this Halloween dark
alone in my skin
unprotected from ghosts/

another born her month/day
returns now same week as she

                              what's happening?

back from the jazz funeral
i gave him in blood ink
death he insisted on
pulled off once more
ghost of a mother's misaimed need
ghost of Vietnam of himself
poet of ghosts i wept over
& cursed called husband:

                              what's happening?

sisters

the city is screaming with sirens
this mother's day...
mine calls me sister
word for daughter   lost/
unintentional a rebuke
for years of neglect.,,

i am an expatriate from brooklyn
working my way home
thru who & where
in bassetts outdoor cafe / tribeca...
my mother is standing victorious in her wheel chair
two flashing silver swords
charging into battalions of yarn
setting traps for unnamable demons...
maybe not   quite the way it is
in the nursing home where i left her
but the image persists
trembling hands struggling
against the odds

to keep busy...pass time

she always said;
words   my business
i cannot make those unique spreads
i once hid away
covering my bed   chairs
shawls & ponchos i wear
for warmth   especially
when it's hot
& the chill is most cruel
to a solitary woman's flesh...

"my eyes are bad...i gave notice
to the head boss   it's time i retire"

she looks at some photographs i took
on her 90th birthday
who's the old woman in the wheel chair?
she asks...

i ordered some yarn from a catalogue
i hand her
 one more   a sweater   for me please

one more poem
to weave her thread with my words on a page
shroud what came before

one more

Linda Lerner

Three Excerpts from THE CORPSE IS DREAMING #20

johnnie
& the way shed used to write it
was w/ie instead of y at the end
just like my real mother did
sometimes it felt like I was her son
but when we did it I was her daddy even tho she was older
& I never saw the black slug rising
like a night sun behind me
I wanted to
I wanted to
god how I wanted to
but at the last minute I think I chickened out & turned away
I don't know why
I wish I did
I wish I knew what my neck muscles know
& knew from the beginning
the dark in there is calling & calling & calling
the meat dark in there is calling for dillinger
& also for johnnie
if lawrence knew he'd tell me
oh yes I know he wd
but he's gone away
maybe into the sky
maybe into the clouds in the sky
maybe into the alley

lawrence's mask is worn so thin death wd see straight thru to where I
was crouching inside
dillinger
I promise not to eat you
& I won't huff or puff or blow yr bones down
death has always been such a rotten liar
death can do almost anything but he can't tell the truth
I've known for a long time he's been in love w/dillinger
just like my father
but not being able to find dillinger has sent death into fits & rages
& frenzies

death gets down & froths at the mouth & rolls around on the ground
like a dog
& those places he has touched is where the earth cracks open
& I'm not sure where dillinger's gone
I used to be him
I used to own his name
I used to wear dillinger's legs & face & arms
& dillinger's hands were my gloves
& dillinger's feet were my shoes
& dillinger's cock was always slapping against my

legs
tho now it's shriveled & quiet in the dark tent of my trousers
& now
something is black & rising
it spreads a night fire all thru my blood
& when it enters me it eats a big hole where it punches thru
are you my father lying w/me beneath the soiled sheet on the black
sidewalk
or am I sleeping w/the other

I don't know why this dying lets me taste my own body
lets me taste the dirt on my lips
lets me know the sour taste of skin
lets me taste the black aura that sleeps w/my body
& the aura is dying
the aura knows that it is dying
I can feel the way its breathing is getting lower & lower
& I want to hold it in my arms & rock it to sleep & make it not go
away
& the aura won't let me even tho I can hold it its darkness keeps

slipping thru my cooling flesh like a thin bruised cloud that wants
to float into the sky
can you hear it calling dillinger
lawrence   where are you
the call is really a kind of frenzied cry that fades to a language I
never heard spoken before
& where is the other
I thought I was dreaming
my words were a movie in the biograph theater
I saw them
I was sitting w/polly
or maybe it was anna before she was billie
& we were both eating popcorn
& each other

when her whole body entered mine
not just the sex parts
but everything
& we were floating in the warmth of each other's juices
calling for anna
billie
polly
to come home to my body
come home to my name
& my laugh & my money & my arms & my mask & my face & my dreaming &
my dance & my cars & my veins & my guns & my love
& I didn't know I cd taste my body the way I cd taste a cookie & I
want the taste to linger
something w/a little chocolate in it
maybe some whipped cream too
funny
I remember the word but can't find the taste
can't locate the memory it's stuck in

Todd Moore

Four from BOURBON SKIN # 21

reasons for getting off at the wrong stop   3.25.98

there are cracks in the glass
where the light turns flaxen
i'm looking for evidence
of (you love me)
dissect reflection
blank stare meets mine there
what are you saying
with brown cast down

i have studied you mirrored
extended my focus
read your ambivalence
like a technical journal
but each lesson returns
me to things i can't learn
i'm marooned on conclusions
that kindle more questions
desperate this loving
i've laid soft beside you
hardening myself
to make it easier slowly
but ease puts a veil up
loving isn't simple
we are complex people
made to contradict ourselves

now the subway removes me
from your flat in chicago
where we've laid and lied
and lingered
thinking one of us should go
climbed on this train together
and are slicing through the tunnels
you're trying to avoid my eyes
i snatch yours from the window

there are cracks in the glass
but i'm looking past them
pressing your expression
for some sign of sincerity

you are shifty and silent
stifled and violent
angry at yourself
for what you thought you had and didn't

i am straining the sound of the subway
from your breathing
straining your image reflected for something
besides the graffiti
some sign that you love me
i am straining my awareness
of the facts to spare my feelings

there are cracks in the glass
that refract your reflection
i'm looking for evidence
senseless inspection
i'm searching your face there
while you stare at nothing
so much nothing reflecting
while you look away

Jacqueline Kras

God Is the Rust Inside of You

God is the rust inside of you
that flecks each gesture with grime,
initials that appear on fogged glass,
that smell of rotting floors in subway restrooms.

God is the sound of old feet
that tip-toe on wet pavement
into bars that don't close.

Not calendar scenery,
but always in the faces of abandoned mines,
like yours.

God laughs tornadoes.

Bath

Let me wash her off you
with my soap flesh and sponge hair.
Back and forth and back and forth.

Mascara'd lashes,
little whips to scrub your cheek and chin.
A pumice tongue to rub away worn pledges
and steel wool kisses to scour doubts.

Let the honeysuckle, lavender and lilac
douse her drugstore incense.
Let me rinse off her film with a rain of talc.
Let me sop her up with this towel of skin
and polish you with this sheet of flesh.

Let me pour my name onto you.

Dog

If I remembered to notice you,
you remembered to nuzzle,
to burrow,
to lick my selfish hand.

Lucky, King, Rex.
Any name and you ran drooling.

Your eyes star in some nightmares;
or do cameos in dreams.

My mending memory plagues me.

Frances LeMoine

Three from PAPER HEART 3 #22

RED PETALS

Like the curved blade
of a Samurai
I dream of pushing
my sword deep
into my love's scabbard
while scented petals
delicate and yielding
quiver
and drop
to the ground.

The moon is reflected
in the black water
of the well
its face half-obscured.
by the fallen blossoms of
yesterday's beauty.

The garden path
washed by my tears
will soon be
covered with
a blanket of red and
yellow.

The day does not come easily.

KAREN

I dreamed of you
Your head cocked towards me
as if gauging my every
weakness
analyzing my vulnerability

to your charming ways
like so many years ago
after you left the hospital
your time of sadness
behind you
and mine
just beginning.

CORAZON

The walking stick,
leaning in the corner, knows it.
And, so do I: the wanderlust
beckons.

Soon enough -
you're silhouette in the doorway,
slipping my embrace,
the long shadow,
the creaking gate,
the final wave at the crest
of the hill.

The wind that whistles
through the treetops
will bring nothing
but the memory
of your sighs.

Though I will search the sky
for a message, I will
find only clouds, feathers,
dust, pale light and a hint of winter
(but no trace of you).

Now it begins
this season of long shadows
and the silence of stone.

RD Armstrong

Three from BLUE COLLAR WORK #23

For Sammy

Don't ask me
why the poems
pour out,
why I record
ballads of
sad cafes,
the wind,
the rain, &
hell, who is
to judge
the depth
of darkness
when the lamps
are blown out
in the Sad Cafes
along the coast,
like Sammy
who always run
I am gushing out inside,
spilling
my literary
guts, & when
I am on a
downward
glide
I become
a gypsy moth
that I
can never
ever catch.

Daily Bread

A Natural History of the Blues,
early to bed down a winding corridor
& dancing no more to big bands a'plenty:
a woman has her fruit to sell,
a man has nothing save
his dignity.

The Preacher said we can't
put Creation in a box or bottle, then
there are hurricanes passing through the Gulf,
the small sailboats tossed aside,
the old rock piers of New England
& vulnerable roads not taken.
Where the literary sidewalk ends.
Where a Holy League of Nations adjourns
to extend moral judgment,
to choose the Blue & Gray ornaments of tomorrow.
In these rooms water wears the stone thin.
Each backbone is curved from years of waiting.
And the rest of the Outlaw Planet, Earth,
stagger around inside themselves.
The ashes of Tara simmer on horizon.
If the clock has stopped, what time is it?
Across the way one red light blinks on
then off again. If I am but
a solitary man encamped
here in this time, this place,
who shall bear me away
from the mournful evening traffic?
And who shall inherit my loss,
who shall open the files
of my vault & liquidate
the journals of my struggles?
Ribs of white-oak press in closer.
Sweet Jesus, a thousand mortgaged souls
hug the land-side of your Castle,
those who remain & a few
drifters from other
outback regions
where the windows of
their foursquare houses are streaked
with starshine & a magic lantern
glitters in the mountains,
a rusty lizard feigning death,

most of the whitewashed cabins
remaining empty. A dog barks
& a diesel engine roars to life,
remindful of the great resourcefulness
of change & the heavy ox-child
of the journey, another
spiritual dry spell of amnesia
& the long farewell of friendship.
The Army of the Potomac has clay feet.
There is only one universal language
& stragglers carrying silence.

I Truly Am Long Gone & Far Out

I truly am
long gone & far out,
one of the best married men
of the last few years.

But I'm not that easy to find.
Yeah, yeah, yeah, come on, modus operandi.
It was like I had a rented room in my own hometown.
And a majority of the girls were there, screaming.

Something about hamburgers & sex,
how much of something you can stand, like love,
ooooo, will I (we) ever get back home again,
ain't it amazing, ain't it amazing how
we come undone.

Listen, I'm a plain white boy
consistently Rockin' & Rollin' at The Hop.
Whenever I see sparks fly...
Steamy vocals from Saturday night.
And we'd go into town, later,
for a Coke.

Nothing to it
but stress & turmoil,

since I broke up with Peggy Sue.
You know how it is to be alone
& want someone.

"It's OK," they say, to the troops.
And I move among them with a sly smile,
drinking my precarious poison like
it was cold draft beer.

And the room spins again
& my smile fades away & I am
Just Plain Ol' Guitar Slim marching
on to Doomsday. The Earth
is flat all over, I believe,

& I am too involved
in war.

Errol Miller

Two from NOMADS OF OBLIVION #25

In the House of Original Sin

In the House of Original Sin
everybody is a winner
although the plot is kind of
hazy and hard to figure
if God created everything in the beginning
then he or she created Satan or the Devil
and yet according to the director of
the movie God (he or she or it) gets
mad every now and then for the weakness
in us paltry humans, he or she gets
angry for humans falling prey to the
wicked ways and means of this aforementioned
Satan or Devil fellow (or woman)
but if indeed God created everything
and that means he or she created Satan
then I guess it eventually means he
takes it out on the pale humans for
supposedly giving in to one of
God's own creations...and if God
created not only Satan but the paltry
humans who piss God off by playing
in Satan's sandlot, well, I guess
God is just a schizo like all of us
and doesn't figure he is taking it
out on us for playing some of the
tunes God put on the jukebox in
the first place...and don't give
me that specious junk about it all being
some kind of a test, because if God created
everything, which some of those movies claim,
there is no reason to keep making up odd
spur of the moment quizzes, everything is
preordained and set up and all the graduate
committees are in place and the dictionaries
are all written up without any possible room

for adding on new words or visions or thoughts
so once again in the House of Original Sin
I guess everybody is a winner because if
God created everything, which the academy
award winning screenwriter says, then
he created the buxom woman who took the
bite out of the apple that the serpent gave
her and God also created the serpent who
brought the damn apple...I have nothing
against apples, in fact they are good for
you on a diet, and I never really hung out
with serpents, except now and then the two
legged kind, but once again I think God
needs to see some kind of a shrink and get
a little focused, it's like a kid building
a house out of playing cards, then creating
matches with which to put this house on fire
and then this same kid invents a fire truck
and fire men and a whistle and he begins to
get red in the face blowing on the whistle and
screaming Help Help Fire Fire Fire
It's just too complicated sometimes for
a paltry weak human as myself to
deal with. In the House of Original
Sin everybody is a winner
Hallelujah

1/22/95

Hymn for nameless children

And the dust laughed
And the crying animals said we love you
I know where your heart hurts
the wound is a civilization
that has no interpreter
You will allow me to put my ear down against the burn
i will trouble you very little when
i sing your elementary school's favorite
marching song to

the black holes collapsing
over my shoulder
And the train station was swallowed
by the smoke of the engine of the train
when it said I love you
in the hidden language of the new dawn
when children were butter on the end of
dangerous adult knives
and the lunch crowd would always be standing on line in some
hard to pronounce town
where death was so easily accepted
And animals cry in tandem while
their parole officers sleep in
because it is a holiday in their bloodstream
and the national monuments of fear
have melted in the new peace accords
of pain

Wander then
with a lost room in your eyes
when we reach the rendezvous of
skin and intent
there will be time for yelling
and shaking off the bewildered shoes
there will be dancing in the
deaf zone
we will become nouns
of trust
waters of dreams
Wander then head first
under the poor sun of
good mourning
Your blood is reckless with love
Your blood is the way we breathe

Scott Wannberg— 5/26/99

Three from BOMBED IN NEW MEXICO #26

waco grabbed

fuller's hat & threw
it to me & fuller
sd you'd better give
it back & waco went
up to the old man
like he had the
world by the ass
& just as he was abt
to give the old
man a slap upside
the head fuller
hooked a knife in
to waco's right
leg & he went oh
mama while i
dropped the hat
when fuller picked
it up & put it
back on he sd never
fuck w/a man's hat
waco was still bent
over when fuller
winked at me & sd
he ain't gonna
die but he'll be
walking real funny

Todd Moore

THESE REVERIES UPON THE SOUND OF A PIANO, ALONE

is it the coffee?
and these dust particles spiraling
    in the shaft of window light?
you've been to the east, and back
somewhere with trees
       and a bird bath
you haven't been back home in years
how much music can they put
         on a compact disk?
this one has been playing for hours
and it's only halfway done
it is the third day of Spring
yesterday was Bach's 312th birthday
--stillness--
i wonder if
it was the heroin Bill Evans used
    that gave him this sense
  of unhurried time?
seems like an eternity....

22mar97

LIKE TU FU

poetry has eluded me for months
i spend the morning painting the window trim
on my house it is the writing that has eluded
me not the poetry i light an incense stick
and have a cup of coffee those poems by Tu Fu
have stuck with me until noon
his neighbor's broken willow tree
wine that dispels a thousand cares
i should call that lady who asked me
to paint her house it is not so important
to write poetry all the time

8june99
Mark Weber

Two Excerpts from ON/OFF THE BEATEN PATH #27

At a gas station in Newberry
Springs Regis Philbin drones
while I buy my first tank of gas
outside L.A.
Nearby
a solar collector station
patiently absorbs sunlight
-- magical conversion near Barstow
land of maroon hoods and freight yard's clang.
High desert rolls off
into the great beyond
rolling up to the base of
burnt igneous rocks
as if swept by ancient sirocco
brooms as if (no carpets
available) ancient sands
from old Route 66 became
fill for jagged volcanic arroyos.
Clusters of rock the color of dried blood
thrust up through this high desert sandbox
like broken teeth on an
upturned jawbone
as if here, the earth is
a battered skull or some part
of a skeletal geology
exposed
to weather.
Magma fingers
stubbed and broken
reaching skyward
surrendering to sun's
indifferent attention.

Interstate 40
Modern highway
four lanes
twice the convenience
of the Hillbilly Highway
Ancient Route 66
the once and future link

Chi-town to EL LAY
two lanes of history
two lanes synonymous with the romance of
THE ROAD

Kerouac
On the Road Again
Bobby Troup
Get your kicks on Rte. six six
Wanderlust
See the USA in your Chevrolet
James Dean
Airstream
Motel 6.

Route 66
shadows I-40
two lanes of cracked
asphalt that keeps
coming back to
haunt the memory
as visions of simpler times
return again and again

Route 66
like some prehistoric
tar-encrusted
Loch Ness monster
appearing out of
desert wilderness
to dog the trail
of I-40 and spook
the traveler with nightmares of
less than a quarter of
a tank of gas and
"next services 55 miles"

Route 66
asphalt serpent
snaking from Barstow
to Needles
through Kingman
to Flagstaff
past Gallup
to ABQ and on
to Amarillo

and Oklahoma City beyond
(where 168 chairs wait for no one).
A red line on the map
cutting into the sandy bottom
of this long-dead sea bed
this forsaken geography
of pulverized rock fields
fossilized trees
lava fields and sandstone.
Unchanged.
Timeless except
for the whimsy and folly
of the Land Lord:
man.

Mesas cling to the distant horizon
as I head east towards NM border.
Mesas of Hopi and Navajo Reservations...
Where coyote trickster first dogged my
trail back in '74
where adventures began and ended
along with meetings of remarkable
men and women: Thomas Banyacya,
Mina Lanza, Sylvia Richards, John
Nomura, Sari Staggs
all but last two gone from this earth
and in some ways
all gone to me now.

And still
something darts
through the scrub.
Some kind of shadow...

Long hours on lonely roads:
the mind wanders around looking
for something to do.
Inevitably, it comes back to the familiar
stripping away the layers of things
onion-like – peeling

back the skins.
I think of Don and Chaparral
and Luis Campos and Todd
Moore and Roger Taus and
John Macker and Mark Weber
and all the other poets I know
(and don't know)
All of them working
quietly laboring away in service of
THE POEM – before work or
after, doing what must be done
so they can continue to make
the holy POEM even if said
holy POEM is just a few sad
lines long.
I'm thinking how the poet
cannot hope to make a living
(unlike other artists) solely from
this craft without dependence
on grants or fellowships or prizes
or teaching or betting on the
horses or trust funds or con games.
Few just write (or exist to just
write) THE POEM.
It's crazy.
I'm crazy.

And yet...

In the god-forsaken badlands
that separate Lupton (to the west)
and Gallup (to the east)
one does not expect to find anything
of note, much less remarkable.
Perhaps it's the way the desert
camouflages its constant state of movement --
hidden from our casual glimpses out
across the seemingly endless nothing –
that sets us up for the next surprise...
A land devoid of definition
a blur of shapes
of dirty / washed-out colors.

And yet
a sudden splatter of
confetti-white

shatters a cool sky –
a cluster of motion
that blinks on...
then off. Then on...
Then off!
It is only a flock
of white birds flying
in a wide circle but
in this endless caged
monotony of road noise
and white line fever
It is an aerial ballet
exquisite.

White freckles against
a blue sky.

Pot holes and the blast of
a semi bring me back to
the business at hand.

RD Armstrong

Six from LOST HIGHWAY #28

robert johnson

soil sifting
through lean
fingers that
pluck those
steel strings
tightened by
bottleneck to
give a sensual
groan that
unchains his
throat cuts
loose his
blues it's
what makes
mud sanctify
blood anoint
watch his
hands his
fingers the
way they
gesture with
the glint of
his eyes call
the skies to
rip loose
the lightning
night for the
devil calling
in his dues

Tony Moffeit

Hoochie Coochie Man
for Willie Dixon

Wolf (as in Howling)
  couldn't read so Willie had to
    read the words that he wrote for him to sing
He'd whisper them into Wolf's ears
    even after months of training Wolf to do them
      Sometimes they'd have a good cut all the way down
and right at the end
    Wolf would turn around and say
        Man I didn't Hear What you said
and mess up the whole damn thing.
    During the World War Two earth gone mad
Willie refused the U.S. government when they came
to induct him
Told them he didn't want to go
as blacks were not citizens but subjects
    Knew how to play his singers off of each other
Would tell Wolf that a particular song was for Muddy
(as in Waters)
when in fact he wanted Wolf to do it
    knowing there was that little thing going on between
them
    Wolf of course would then Howl to do it
okay Hoochie Coochie Man
    i know you
Mellows down
    Easy
when those lights go out
  walking the blues with your little red rooster
the wang dang doodle
built for comfort
just wanna make love to you
sure, Willie
    i hear you there beaming
and whole generations of dance floors
    have learned how you walked and sung it
there in the invigorating soiree of
Hey Now

Scott Wannberg—1/31/92 & 2/4/92

73

CHICAGO

all night
junior wells
buddy guy
southside blues jam
just kids in 1970
and now we listen
to vinyl
pops and cracks
and junior chanting
i just want to
make, make, make, make
love to you
while your back
sweats tough
and strong
i wrap my arms
around and squeeze so
fucking hard
trying to knock
out the poison
and hot
stale air
undiscovered
undiagnosed
inside
and clear away vines
thick
and kiss your neck
and wait for
the next song
to take us back
to our
southside youth

Lawrence Welsh

the poem

was shit
but the
guy backing
the poet
was playing
a sweet
quitar
riff that
had me
searching
for robert
johnson
i knew
the color
of death
in a glass
of bourbon
& swam
in the
black rain
bow of a
colt 32

Todd Moore

Twenty Notes Gone South

remember those beer-stained nights
of rompin', out-of-focus blues
when couples squeezed onto crowded dance floors
to dance the crazy-legged be-bop & jive, or
jumpin' at the woodside, or
doin' the crosstown, las' chance fo' romance-
closing-time boogie.
remember the band hittin' the ninth refrain runnin'
like a roundhouse haymaker findin' its mark

sweating under red and blue lights
while everyone was hypnotized by
the big man on the mic,
always dressed in a suit, Chicago-style
hair slicked back
remember how the big man never took off the shades
even at night, even as he slept, perhaps.
remember how he worked so hard
hunched over
cupping his instrument
pulling it into himself
grunting and shouting
sweat pouring off his brow
blowing his soul into and through
ten-holes
turning twenty notes into a
vocabulary of sighs and moans
like a mile-long, south-bound freight
pulling its tired load of joy and sorrow
over Breakheart Pass.
remember the big man driven
onwards
always

William Clarke is dead
twenty notes gone south, gone
home to rest

let us pause and remember

RD Armstrong

Four from FEEDING THE ANIMAL #31

DOUBLE SECRET OF THE RAIN

In the beginning it was like that:
life, death, all other poems,
began with the rain and the dream.
It is raining softly in the dream, steadily.
There is the discreet music of raindrops.
A clan from the South, from Calabria perhaps,
are exhuming the body of a dead relative.
All are soaked with rain. The women are clothed
in their black Sunday best. The young girls
wear garlands of wet flowers on their foreheads.
One of the girls is being initiated
by the older women, professionals of death,
who draw the cadaver's shiny brown withered arm
across the child's face in a ritual caress.
I look away through the thin veil of rain.
Above the horizon projects
the upper limb of a huge planet.
The page on which I write: it has become enormous,
big as a church-wall, crudely painted white.
The letters of the words are far too large to read,
and the rain streams down across them.

The wet petals drop from the garlands, one by one.
In the beginning it was like this.
Rain falls through the dream of the world,
through a life that even in dreams
never raises its voice.
A life like rain. A death
like a long slow rain.

SMALL CREDO

After nearly sixty years
in this diseased outpost,
I don't believe in
very much,

but I do firmly believe in
mysterious disappearances,
and in the spontaneous combustion
of certain human bodies,
while sitting quietly and alone,
at night, in their
shabby easy chairs.

TREATISE ON BEAUTY: ITS SUDDEN DELIGHT, ITS TRICKS. ITS BLAZING JOY AND TORTURES

How stunning, this hummingbird,
a thrum of green and ruby,
sipping nectar.

Or refine it more: the great Blue Morpho
(Rhetenor, or Achilleus, or Cypris),
its broad blue wings floating, dipping down a silent path
between huge dark tree-walls in Amazonas.
It can amaze, delight the heart --but then,
by the muddy creek-bank, a fluttering carpet of Morphos
dining on the ooze of rotting meat.

And this other thing, this bluebottle,
a glitter of bright metallic blue,
busy with its congenors, feasting on garbage,
laying little white eggs in excrement.
So sharply repulsive, the bluebottle.
Where (in my mind) hides the difference?

Or make it burning and sinister. In sunny Spain,
small and gorgeous green-gold insect
(Lytta Vesicatoria, family Meloidae)
daintily nibbling on leaves of ash and privet:
the Blister Beetle, Cantharidin, yes, Spanish Fly.
Dried, ground to powder, tinctured, and a tiny taste
tickles and inflames the tracts, ignites the flagging passions –
but just a little more can bring
wretched, agonizing death.
Where were we? Was this all about
my mind, my gorgeous waking mind,
which is really not my own?
And that, asleep, my ugly dreams inherit me?

Were we coming to this? To this place of no color,
no gleaming beauty, no heart, no gasp and shudder of grappling flesh?
Just this silent vacancy, everything covered
with the grey dust of desertion?

Bird, butterfly, bluebottle, burning beetle:
to know them, and to know. must I awake
and eat them, one and all? Let them move me as they move
through my famished gut? Well. then. so be it.

TO BE NOTHING, AND FEEL THE WIND

Even back then,
when everyone hitchhiked,
I had a tough time of it.
Too large, too ugly.
Bad eyes, also, no doubt.
Oxnard was awful, but for me
the stretch between Paso Robles
and Camp Hunter Liggett
was always the worst.

Christ, all the hours,
waiting for a ride,
memorizing the dirt at my feet.
In those days I could have written
a pretty fine book:
The Tragic and Marvelous
Roadside Debris of Central
and Southern California.

I never wrote it. But life is kind.
I may have the chance again
in my declining years. Camp
Hunter Liggett is still where it was.

To be nothing, and feel the wind
of the big trucks passing.
Debris: even the word
is beautiful.

John Thomas

Four from FAMILIARITIES #33

Epistles from the Department of Tempting Fate

I am leaving the house where I have raised my children,
harpies out of my womb to borrow the image from Dylan Thomas
Many and busy comings and goings went on here
all the teemings of suburban growing up
The cupboards are full
with the mementos of small happinesses
and the documentations of well-lived afternoons

I can throw out now all these needings
to record just how real and normal it was
how Donna Reed: just what I wanted
the detritus of desire for what couldn't be named predicating itself over and
over in these drawers
If the kids don't want this stuff
and they don't
I can bag it and call the Good Will
It was I who needed the fetishes of a life
dense with familial purpose.
I can chuck now the gymnastics ribbons and soccer trophies
and Bar awards

Such proof of meaning-making is no longer necessary

In the second drawer in the hall closet
in a stretched then broken rubber band
is a bundle of decades of hit-up letters
from the Leukemia Society
I could never throw these away
such potent bad luck charms
tempting the powers of destiny and ruin
to feel rebuffed
unacknowledged
not owed obeisance

I couldn't dare fate just then
in the middle of it
so I bargained for postponement
The growing up is done now and
no one has been lost
not even existentially

Life on the Carpe Diem Model

Perhaps the wise ones
Horace, Spenser, Marvell
meant seize one day
or one hour
or one blessed fleshly communion
once in awhile
That Latin Ode
and Renaissance reprises
intended temporal pillage
the ravish of limited moments
small relishes
every so often
I seem to seize the day
on a continuous basis
it gets a little wearying
to wrap around and hold fast
always
to capture the glories
of each winged flight
every day a new campaign

Patricia Cherin

you can learn so much from historical fiction

my fall booklist for english 390: fiction now
came out with the typo,
"gerald haslam--the wages of sine."

haslam's wages of sin
is a very fine collection of short stories

but one might be tempted to compose
a trilogy of novels
detailing, from a marxist perspective,
the inadequate remuneration of mathematicians
from pythagoras to the present

with its volumes entitled

the wages of sine,
the wages of cosine,
and the wages of hypotenuse.

neither rain nor whatever. . .

four of my best graduate students this year,
among the most intelligent, motivated,
and responsible i've taught in nearly
forty years, and excellent writers to boot,
are all career employees of the postal service.

i don't know whether to attribute this
to the exercise of delivering the mail,
with the subsequent circulation of
oxygen to the brain,
or to the thinking they can do on the job,
or to a qualifying exam that really does
assure a generally well qualified work force.

maybe it's just coincidence.

all i know is that,
although their talents differ in emphasis -
one's more analytical,
one's more the poet,
one's highly erudite and cultured,
one's an indefatigable researcher -

their assignments are always fulfilled
with an eye to quality

and never arrive late.

Gerald Locklin

Three from QUEEN OF BOHEMIA #34

ALLEN! HOWL FOR US WITH YOUR GHOSTLY TONGUE
Elegy for Allen Ginsberg

Allen Ginsberg
Burning shadow
Of Blakean angel
Footprint on
Whitman's grass
Beat of
Kerouac's unchangeable heart
Of Heaven
Allen Ginsberg
Creaking
To Eternity
In William's red wagon

Your voice
Red wind of the moon
Your pen
Candle revealing
The bottom of the sea

Allen Ginsberg
The only author
I happily saw
At the LA Times Book Awards
With holes in his shoes

Oh! Allen
Howl for us
With your ghostly tongue

POEM FOR MY FATHER

His eyes show me things
So small
As to be large
Beyond measure

And now the glistening eye is closed
Now, to his child
Nothing is understood
Without the geography
Of his eye
That he not see, not speak
That the countries of his mind
Should sleep --
Hardly a reality

Now, the world is not enough
The sky, the sea
For it is he who saved it
Again and again
By seeing it

And when he sleeps
The world sleeps
But not as well

COLD ELLISON V

Warm summery days
At the Ellison
And "Bones" the young dog Chris found
In the last stages of starvation
Infested with heartworms
Damaged eye from being kicked
Back full of shotgun pellets
And Chris had to carry him everywhere
Slung across his shoulders like a mink stole
It was beginning to seem that

He was deciding he would spend
The rest of his life on Chris' shoulders
"Bones" is fat now, and trots

Fat lazy days at the Ellison
And the building is finally earthquake-proof
So that with the 7.5 sent from Joshua Tree
And the 3,000 aftershocks
It moved with such grace
Cruised the shocks, the ripples
Like an elegant ship
And it still moves
To the music in Paul and Barb's apartment

And for my son Patrick
(My beautiful son)
And the Blue Crew surfers, these days
The waves are good
At night I walk down to the sea
And in the very place
They ride their boards
Dolphins leap and roll and ride
The waves in, themselves
The very spot
Must be a good one
Warm summer waves

Soft swaying days
At the Ellison
Its marshmallow bricks
The lazy elevator
And my daughter Maureen returns
From Asia (my beautiful daughter)
She brings me a gift
Of a Buddhist temple bell
The bell she gives me
Brings three dreams --

I dream I am a Buddhist monk
And that I have been given
A small zendo
The size of our apartment
I dream I enter a deep dark cave
Where there are Giant Living Buddhas

I dream I am on a

Buddhist monk basketball team
But they have to stop the game
Because we are jumping too high

"Now that's a real dream team"
My daughter says

Soft summer days
At the Ellison
John whispers
Across the room
"You and I, Philomene, that's
All that matters --
You and I"

"You and I, John, and
The radiant, the vast..."
"Apartment", he says
Soft, dreaming days
The Ellison dreaming, swaying
Dipping and sailing
Its own warm seas

Philomene Long

Four from COLD EYE BURNING AT 3AM #35

CRUSHED PIGEON WITH THE SECRET

Crushed pigeon
On the pavement
No head
No breast
A mere gray smudge
With only one wing erect
Moving gently in the
Afternoon breeze

All life and death
Fluttered
In that wing
Gray feathers splayed
It flew
Higher, wider
A wing that seemed to me
Broad enough to cover
All Jerusalem

I sing to it Isaiah's lamentation
"O Jerusalem, Jerusalem,"
"How often would I have gathered
Thy children together even as a hen
Gathered her chicks under her wing
And you would not...
As one whose mother comforts,
So will I comfort you"

Gray cement. Gray pigeon
Life and death at once
The wing a tongue
About to call, to utter
Bringing to this page
The great secret
The word, the world itself

At this very moment

A door slammed behind me in the room
Slammed shut - the door to the poem.

The wing had
Had been writing itself
Opening the word
But only once
Only once
Could not hear it again
Gone
Left with no more
Than what was already known
An impeccable symmetry - life, death

No word
Only that image--
Smashed gray carcass
On a gray road
Above it that gray wing
Swaying in the breeze

But no crushing wheel
No closing door
Can take away
This winged Secret—
Imperishable
Fluttering
Unutterable

Perfect

LOS ANGELES EARTHQUAKE
4:31 A.M. JANUARY 17, 1994

The earth, too, is afraid
I tell you
The earth is afraid
There are far greater earthquakes
In the depths through which
It palpitates
Far deeper black

4:31 A.M.
First the roar
Then out the window I see Venice
Rock in the enormous unseen arms
It looks like the end of the world

I stand in the middle of the room
Now a profound black
All I see are my bare white feet
Beneath them the floor is invisible
Only a blind rage of waves
The language of cataclysm
A crucifixion of winds
It is as if all that exists
Are these black winds
And my bare white feet
Which I am surprised to see
Begin to glow
Glowing, floating above a sea
Of endless night
This cemetery of space
Nightbloom of terrors
Even the breath crumbles
In this tomb of blind eyes
This mirage of deepest black
This terrible hoof of God

As I watch my iridescent feet
The movement stops
Naked, fragile
I reach for my crucifix
Draped only in the large black nun's cross
I, now, a bride
Of the slow, trembling Eternity

The earth, too, is afraid
Naked, fragile
That God is unfathomable
That our shouts
Do not turn the world
That heaven and earth
Will be smashed in the darkness
And pass away

POEM FOR MY MOTHER

Sometimes I feel I can hear her
When I write a poem

When it ends
She is gone

I am always reluctant
To end a poem

EVERY POEM I WRITE

Every poem I write
Is a suicide

It will say
"I am your death
Hidden in a spasm
Of clay

Dazzling, ferocious
Now only a
Flame in your hand."

Philomene Long

Three from NEW SHOUTS AT BROKEN DREAMS #36

FROM A BUICK 6— REVISITED

if you're cracked up
it's denver
or el paso
and the dark-light mamas
of now
returning
from engagements
of mind/body
separation
and declarations
of financial irresponsibility

can i borrow
borrow
your cab of nothingness
a $20 retrospective
a nightmare
of over drawn lucidity

someday i'll strut
that way
and unload the victims
of the gut bucket
reality
victims
of the aluminum block
serenade

THE QUEEN OF ODESSA

the queen of odessa
is limping
her leg crushed
by an uninsured
trucker

a metal rod
like a cane

the stench of
petrochemicals
in her hair

the hometown theater
star of
bride of frankenstein
picnic
splendor in the grass

weeps on the side
of the road

she's holding a
cardboard sign:
anywhere but here
anywhere but Odessa

THE RETURN OF PANCHO VILLA

Ruly's talking about
Pancho Villa
as he finishes
a six buck cut
and genuflects for
the business

It's survived since
the '60s
and now they're all

back
listening
hiding out
Candelario Cervantes
Pablo Lopez
Francisco Betran
$1,000 reward
dead or alive
in Albuquerque
New Mexico
but this is El Paso
Texas
Ruly's Barber Shop
a $5,000 reward
buried
somewhere
for Francisco Pancho Villa
last seen
riding down
Interstate 10
heading west

Lawrence Welsh

Three from LATE NIGHT ON THE PSYCHE WARD #37

September 5

Peter is back after only 8 days.

He was caught directing traffic, naked,
claiming to be Charlie Manson and Hitler.
He's sunburned, scratched up.
His feet are cracked and cut
from walking barefoot.
His voice is garbled, sounds like he's barking
with a mouth full of gravel.
But he continues dropping lists at the desk.
Some lists tell us who he is: "a homosexual and a lesbian
and Zar governor of Andromeda Strain..."
Some tell us diseases he wants cured: "Soviet's tongue,
Heineken's turmoil, defecation rot..."
Other lists tell us who he wants
at his "ordination breakfast"
where "wurlitzer coffee" is to be served.
He wants Clinton, Popeye, Queen of England,
Daffy Duck, Mortimer Snerd, King Tut...
In the past he's told me
he sold dope to Jerry Garcia,
shot up with Grace Slick.
Said he likes "combo shotgun"
and rattled off a list of drugs.
He showed me "tracks" on his arm.
But I didn't see much, two or three red dots.
And I just got his toxicology screen results.
Negative for all drugs.
His problem is his brain.
Schizophrenic for 50 years.

He's basically harmless.
Claims to be God-fearing
and---God.

January 6

My tech tells me

back when he did all the street drugs
he knew Richard Ramirez,
the serial killer.
They were from the same barrio.
He also knew a necrophiliac
who worked in a morgue
on the night shift.
He "did" all the dead women
who came in.
All ages, shapes and colors
turned him on.
When he saw a good looking live woman
he'd say, "I wouldn't mind
having her dead."

My tech before this one
said he was in a gang
from ages 14-19,
killed some people,
spent some time in jail.
Left the gang life
when his brother was killed.

Maybe it's true
that people who work in psych
are all ex-wackos themselves,
which begs a question
I don't care to answer.

March 13

"Do you believe in angels?"

my charge nurse asks.

"I don't know," I say.
"Reason tells me no.
Romance tells me yes."

As if blanking out
half my answer he asks,
"Do you think everything
revolves around reason?"

Sensing his Catholic dogma
unchallenged noticeably
by thought, I say,
"Obviously not. We hardly ever
believe anything,
see anything
or hear anything reasonable,
especially here."

Silence.

Silence is golden.

Belinda Subraman

An Excerpt from BAKERSFIELD '99 #38

i worked as a line cook
barely two hours a day
hung out in the bar
after the lunch rush
watched the cooks
blow smoke into the
bent rays of the sun,
while we sipped fools gold.
i watched the line cook here
sit at the stool
pulling back nicotine
and caffeine for
minimum wage—
my eyes fell outside
like rubber balls
dropped from a child's hand
tumbled awkwardly into
the early morning traffic, where
this working reality slid by,
a double breasted suit
with a cell phone,
secretaries, bus drivers,
waitresses with their
heavy tongues and
hands of frogs.
it was the motion
i was interested in,
for a brief instant
everything was pushing
by at remarkable speeds.

i wandered to the bathroom
and saw
purpose sitting in the bar,
he was a forty year old man
that looked sixty.
purpose had a big brass
pinky ring
and a colombo trench coat
over tan slacks.
he carried his money
in a big sterling silver
turquoise money clip

and made a point
to pull it out many times
to run his fingers over
for no particular reason.
he was drinking his
manhattan slowly.
i only thought once
about asking him
where he'd been.

as i left lyon's
i noticed how nothing
here welcomed my arrival,
the muddy grass
the bleak trees
standing in the parking lot
as the dead child sun
stared at me
like a rape victim,
i turned my back
and opened the door
thinking about my interview,
my skin flaked off like ashes
which fell to the pavement
memory came along
to sweep them up.

the name plate read:
SAL LOPEZ,
Attorney at Law,
on both sides
of the name plate
there were pearls
that were his eyes.
his secretary wore
too much make up
her teeth were
yellow from coffee,
just like mine.
sal had black curly hair
and a nice suit.
he looked over my resume
the first five minutes
without saying a word.

"HELL, the only reason
i asked you down here
was as a personal favor

to your old boss
Jane Jensen,"
staring through me.

"uh…thanks?"

"that and your resume,
college degree?"

"yep."

"…and this cover letter
there's poetry on here,
did you know that?
did you do this
yourself?"

"uh-huh…" swallowing.
"you did?…"
he didn't speak again
for another
five minutes.

after a series of
deep breaths,
"well you've got the experience
and the references,"
he said to the wall.
"but you aren't as cute
as the woman
you're going up against."
he said this wanting
me to laugh,
i swallowed again
looking him in the sockets

"i don't know,"
he stands up
walks over to the window
and turns his back
to me to look
out the liquid glass.
i was sweating.
there's no question
in my mind
about doing this job.

Lindsay Wilson

Three from PISS TALKS #39

Promenade

The wood-strawberries
picked
in 1964
between
the remaining
railroad tracks
from
Weimar
to
Buchenwald
tasted
great,
even
without
whipped
cream.

My little gas-chamber

Oh dear
sweet
little
Jesus,
just
give me
a sweet
little
gas-chamber
to put
in it,
just for fun,

all those
Swiss officials
and other
well-to-do
people
who handed
weird
people
over
to those
who
ran
those real
big
gas-chambers

Scars

Four scars in my belly
One in my face
And one on my knee -
But nobody
Can count the scars
In my soul

Harry R. Wilkens

Three from DEATH AND TRANSFIGURATION COCKTAIL #40

The Slaughterhouse 5

Red Wine and Morphine

They weren't your
garden variety
backwoods Okies
night driving
the 4 by 4
backroads by full
moon light,
singing along
to Country Western
hits, hitting the tape
player Auto Rewind
for another go at,
She Got the Gold
Mine and I Got
The Shaft, taking
deep pulls on
the homemade
extra fortified
Lake Country Red,
ghost riding
20,000 head to
a round up for some
imaginary OK Corral
for steers, driving
out of control,
trying to make up
for the worst kind
of lost time,
the kind no clock
can measure.

Zipperhead

Stolie, Chambord and Club Soda

The last loud mouth
red neck that wandered
into his space and
remarked something to
the effect of, "What horror
movie were you the star of
that they didn't need
to use makeup?"
wore his pieced together
jaw with matching wire
to bone braces and a permanent
longneck Bud facial impression
as a permanent reminder
to keep his thoughts to
himself all those long,
cold, solitary nights,
a man might drink in shadows
no outside light could fill.

The Black Hole

Stolie Orange flavored by a drop of
Black Haus, shaken and served up
with a wedge of licorice garnish

He looked as if
his brain had
been sand blasted
clean of all
thoughts, memories
& ideas, all
the blood drained
from his body &

replaced by
a liquid that
smelled vaguely
of formaldehyde,
claimed to be
a true denizen
of the night
in need of
the elixir of
life, sat smoothing
out an incredibly
wrinkled Gold
Certificate twenty
dollar bill
on the scarred
surface of the bar
with an inane
grin on his face
that seemed to
suggest he expected
service sometime
in the not too
distant future.

Alan Catlin

Three from POEMS OF THE ROYAL CONCUBINE LI XI #41

Moon, Stars, Frost

Her entire life under the eye of the moon
this autumn frost lies on earth and mourns
what will become of her at dawn.

Her contest with the stars determines
who is more beautiful. When I look
toward the night sky I feel the light
of thousands of years reach my skin.

But when I look across the meadow
and see the intricate spiderwebs
covered with frost I think of the designs
that have been right here forever.

Looking up again a thousand geese
move south over miles of water.

The Long Walk

The road turned, mountains grew smaller.
The backdrop moved back and forth.
Walking the plains an old man joined my left.
We went a ways without speaking before he said,
"I've seen the battles of warlords,
but this is the worst." I kept silent
thinking he was a spy. Then he said
something that slapped my face:
"gods will play Gods, boys will be boys.
The sad thing is both end up butchering children."

Unfastened Sash

This morning, after washing my hair,
I knotted the sash around my waist
and walked into the perfumed spring garden.
You were there, standing in silk,
watching the pond with your hands on your hips.
When I approached you spoke of the blossoms and how fresh they smelled.
Seeing me blush I went chill with your hot tongue in my mouth.
Right there, with the spill of flowers
on damp earth, your lips moved to my breast
and my sweetened nipple burst into fever.

Leonard J. Cirino

Three from PAPER HEART 4 #42

THINGS I NOTICE #4
Jacaranda's lilac blush
sultry under a gray
watercolor sky

Four crows in a line
one riding shotgun
cut diagonally through
the late-morning air

In the oil field wasteland
marsh grass bows
away from sheets of rain
a crane contemplates
its wrinkled reflection

Late afternoon blues drifts
in with wind's eastbound rush
fickle storm blunders
through town

A wild heart calls
the world turns
as if to look

it's spring
and the search
for love
continues.

VACANCY

There was no vacancy
in fact the whole place had been shut down
locked up
the contents of each room
covered with sheets
shades drawn
doors shut
locked
The paint is peeling
the foliage
dying
A fine layer of dust
covers
all.
I will clean the old place up
make it livable
again.
Slap some paint on
open the windows
unlock all the doors
air it out
Get out the "Murphy's"
clean, clean, and clean some more.
Clean and polish
the old sign
so you'll know
There's a vacancy
You're room is all ready
bed made up
flowers
fresh picked
on the nightstand
The register is open
and ready for you to sign in.
The staff
ready to serve you.

"Do you have any baggage?"

OCCASIONAL LOVER

Afterwards
Taking in the room
I stop at the shrine of pictures
on your bureau:
family, the family dog
the soon-to-be-ex-husband
But no sign that I was ever here
no trace of my impact on you
except an unmade bed and
you coming out of the bathroom
looking flummoxed and happy.

I want my legacy to be more
than a sly smile that fades
over coffee and toast
More than walls that echo with the
passions of the desperate and lonely
More than a brief memory painted
on the breath of night evaporating
like the dew at sunrise.

Raindog

Three from A GATHERING GLANCE LRB #43

SEA CREATURES

for Marty

Sturdy as a bollard, she crouches
beside a tide pool. Lug soles grip rock
slippery with braided ribbons
and air-puffed bulbs of just-flung seaweed.

With the gentle stroke of a mother's finger
on baby skin, she stirs the cupful of life
caught in the salt crusted rock bowl.
Raises eyes brimming Pacific green.

On her back, snug in the rising wind,
her first-born, late-born daughter sleeps.
Only days from her swim in mother
fluid, the infant cells fill with fresh sea air.

For this pair the swirl of the tide
is hardly distinguished from their heartbeats,
skin drenched with ocean spray, rinsed in falling rain,
as natural to them as tea by a landlubber's fire.

WALK OF THE ONE-BREASTED WOMEN

A strange congregation,
these warrior women
creating our own modern myth.
Feet clunky in Reeboks
we march down Main Street,
less interested in destination
than in being.
Hairless heads helmeted
in turbans, wigs and baseball caps
(full heads of hair
follow rites of passage).
Not all are one-breasted.

Some have no breasts, others
a sad little half, or large pinch
taken out of the fullness.
Each carries a shield,
tiny ribbon loop in pink
pinned on the front of her shirt.
Most have taken poison
to drive out the invader, all
live with the sense of time racing.
On this day we join together,
pool our ages, strength,
our hearts. Watch as people
on the streets join in.
By the end of the walk
we're all laughing with joy,
send a glow of hope heavenward
in a cloud wrapped with pink.

MRS. COYOTE

Town knows her
as Mrs. Coyote. Tall and lean,
she lopes through Gold Rush Country
in tawny sweaters with earth
stained pants, her sharp nose
twitching in thought.
Grieved by the western habit
of draping coyote carcasses
over fence posts, unconvinced
their marauding brothers
get the hint, her main concern
is the wildness in their cells.
She sees these untamed eyes
staring out of poets.
Poets, who must be left undisturbed
to record the unwritten songs
that rustle dry grass,
whip treetops into leaf storms,
frenzy incoming tides.
Who express the wildness
in cells stifled long.

Patricia Wellingham-Jones

Two from RAINING ALL OVER #44

Ode to Exxon

I am he as you are he as you are me and we are all together.
See how they drown in the slick black scum,
see how they writhe, I'm crying.
Sitting on an iceberg waiting for the end to come.
Corporation Exxon, stupid bloody money, man you been a naughty boy you
ran your tank aground.
I am the deadman, they are the yesmen I am the walrus.
GooGooGooJoob
Shifty politicians screwing pretty little businessmen in the
boardroom.
See how they lie like fish on their backs
see how they come
I'm crying I'm crying I'm crying.
Coagulating ooze dripping from a dead seal's eye.
Crabpots fishnets penetrating pipeline boy you been a busy girl, why don¹t
you leave us alone.
I am the deadman, they are the yesmen I am the walrus.
GooGooGooJoob
Sitting on an Arctic tundra waiting for the midnight sun,
if the sun don¹t come you get a tan from swimming in the Bering Sea.
I am the deadman, they are the yesmen I am the walrus.
GooGooGooJoob
Exxon Texans smoking cigars don't you think the seagull screams at you?
Scree scree scree!
See how they fly, like birds in the sky, see how they die.
I'm crying.
Money grubbing fishmongers climbing up the Exxon ladder.
Corporation penguins singing Armageddon man you should have seen them
rape
THE LAST FRONTIER.
I am the deadman, they are the yesmen we are the walrus.
GooGooGooJoob

The Snake

The first snake was the snake of man
His soft underbelly so smooth and cool
      yet impenetrable
Sliding up round one of my long legs
I was an apple tree
      drawn to perfection by a man--
      Aristotle/Da Vinci/Michelangelo/Hefner
Freud stole the apple, hiding it in my dreams of Lethe
And I wept as chocolate kisses fell from my mouth

As children my brother and I caught worms from a stray   cat
As legend has it, the worms snaked through our bodies, stealing,
      licking up all of our moisture with their grey tongues
We grew feverish as cracks sprouted
      across the parched earth of our foreheads

The parasitic snake like the dream undreamed
      is always with me
He is part of my living flesh
He forces me again and again to the tree
The hard red fruit falls upon the grass to rot
My long black hair falls
      covering my nakedness like the wind's hush
I cry out for winter
      even as I kiss the dying crocuses with my fingertips
I feel the snake moan in his lethargy
      moan as the leaves begin to fall
      and he knows he must soon leave the flowers and light
      must penetrate the earth now
      in late August
      while the soil is yet supple and giving
          if we both are to survive.

Rebecca Morrison

Three from AMERICAN CHILD #45

an hour before

sept 11 2001

early morning
not a cloud in
the sky

squirrels hop
from branch
to branch

twigs snap
frost crawls
just above the
roots

billie holiday said
"blues is kind of a
mixed up thing - -
you just gotta
feel it"

- - autumn approaches

9/11//2001

american child

"the world is built on a tilt & every loose marble rolls into america" --
- - - - - anatole brombee - - - - -

i am the child of america
the sierra madres are bleeding
i am america
the mad & the magnate marry
the factory wolf howls
i am america
the mantra rumbles with the kinds & the cripples.

i am america
the baby is diced up in dinty moore stew
the lamb is hung by the machinery at noon
the newspapers are shouting from sea to sleazy newspaper sea.
      i am swingband
      i am penitentiary
the highway snakes into the asshole of heaven
      i am jazzpoem
      i am the system
      i am the bells of extinction
      i am the american dream.

i am america
the soup kitchens are swarming
porno talkshows & paparazzi have passioned the brain
buddha in the suburbs --- crack on the plains
& the breakfast of champions has gone insane
& the angels are hunkered up in the whorehouse
of the honkytonk queen.

i am the american dream
i am astrology
i am the burning ghat carrying the ghost of mark twain
down the flowers of the mississippi
mama's in the diner
the hobo's on the cross
let freedom ring
from the sand of sams club to the halls of home depot
to the lines of burger king.

& i am america
death to the jukebox
death to the traveling circus
death to the visions piled in the alley
death to lewis & clark.

i am prophecy
death the pioneers
death to jerry springer
death to the manifest destiny.
i am the dog of hope
death to the trail of tears & of schemes
death to the wildman wandering the alleghenies
death to the gypsy storefront leading to eternity
death to the terror on the tongue of the internet nightmare

death to louis l'amour.
i am the american dream.

& i am the final territory
& i am the state that will someday be
death to the explorers
       the cowboys
         showgirls
        gayblades
        truckers.
death to new zion
       empire state
       golden state
       pilgrim state
& death to the tickertape parade
& death to the promised land
death to utopia.

i am brooklyn
i am el dorado
i am electric chair
i am the chairman
      home run
      atomic waste dump
      ellis island
i am joe dimaggio
i am thomas jefferson.

death to the capitalist
death to the communist
      the anarchist
      the antichrist
      the atheist.

i am levittown
    boystown
    & los alamos
i am the grizzly
    the rabbi
    & the gospel
i am sojourner truth
    geronimo
    & benedict arnold
i am the shithouse the flophouse & the padded room

i am einstein mickey mouse & chief joseph
i am the first & the last man on the moon.

i am the child of america.

i am beauty
i am invention
i am wonder
i am the united fruit company
i am promontory point pikes peak & mai lie
i am the glory i am the savior
i am the black tide of the acid sky

i am the child of america.

i am the magic eagle rising from the smoke
of the terminal explosion
i am the song of indian blood sweeping in the
belly of the canyon
i am the armed guard of patriot children
weeping at the foot of the holy mountain

i am the child of america.

i am humanity
i am fool
i am genius

i am the child of america.

i am the kind of heaven & of hell
i am the ballad of the last romantic
i am the arithmetic eyes of the bureaucrat robot

i am the child of america.

i am the feral infant dancing on the freakstage
of the final sunset

i am the child of america.

labor day/2000

pulling into the garage at night

the things i might have said

that fine dust
that once was me.

the miraculous powder
that once congealed
as a soul,

the memory
that once played
1st violin
among an orchestra
of angels - - -

now battles
for its place
on line
in the supermarket
of an afterlife.

all the important things
i might have said

will argue among themselves
on smiling lips

after i am dead.

normal

One from L. A. RHAPSODY #46

VELOCITY

I.

The velocity of a bullet
is computed by distance
traveled (also known as
space) then divided by time.

The velocity of being on the
receiving end of said bullet
can also be determined
but once received is hardly
worth the calculated effort.

Furthermore, the argument
that my bullet is faster than
your bullet hardly matters
if you are the one being shot.

II.

The velocity of a rainbow
includes color plus the pot
of gold at the end of it.

Whereas a bullet has an
intended target a rainbow
always appears to be an
accident of nature. This is
usually never repeated
except once when driving
from Palm Springs 3 (three)
rainbows magically sprouted
simultaneously from the sky.

Awestruck, we (as a race) like
to be hit by rainbows. They do
not hurt or puncture and always
make you feel lucky or blessed.
Additionally, there is nothing
frustrating about rainbows as
they are not known to kill.

III.

The velocity of a blowjob
must be gauged by the amount
of flourish and embellishment
as practiced by the artist.

Thus oral interpretation
and its variances inevitably
increase velocity with the
intended target being orgasm.

Tangibles like length and girth
divided by time of intended
approach to orgasm plus
above factors provide speed
of said blowjob.

Finally, there are other factors
or qualities when entered into
the equation such as lip thickness
tongue adeptness, depth of activity, etc.
help determine the proper ratios
of time and motion.

But being on the receiving end
of a blowjob is much like being
on the receiving end of a bullet
-- who really cares about its velocity.

IV.

The velocity of friendship
is easily and readily figured
without disturbing factors
of weather or acts of god.

The speed of friendship
is simply determined
by acts of profundity
mixed with consistency
divided by reliability
plus most importantly
the willingness to take said bullet
whatever its velocity
for said friend.

Larry Jaffe

Two from THE BARBIE POEMS
VOL. ONE #47

BARBIE FEELS ABANDONED, IGNORED AND DOESN'T KNOW WHY

it's not because
she's overweight
or doesn't use the
right deodorant.
She's got nice
clothes, a sweet
smile, doesn't
talk too much, is
a good listener.
She's never attacked,
isn't loud, does
not gossip. She's
flexible, has
perfect skin, hair
you could braid
or comb, wrap
around you. You
can have her
sleep with you
or put her in
the closet or
giver her away: do
what only you could
imagine to her.
She'll wait, naked,
patient, never
make a stink

BARBIE FEELS HER LIFE IS LIKE A HOTEL

sterilized, a
facade that
looks shiny
but open the
drawers and
what was wait-
ing, so inviting,
is empty. She
remembers Liv
Ullman wrote
that coming back
from a flight
with all the
lights on it's
as if life goes
on in other
houses. Her
belly could
have a seal
over it like
paper on a
toilet which
doesn't mean
much. She is
the one always
in the Hyatt
Regency elevator
plunging up, out
of reach in a
glassed in case
others notice
but can't touch

Lyn Lifshin

Two from THE BARBIE POEMS
VOL. TWO #48

BARBIE'S OVER 35

the men were horrified, a doll with breasts,   many
men couldn't take it. Mothers wiped me off
the shelf. My hips tilted forward. Some say I had a
sinister look, a villainous smile, not the insipid, stupid
dazed grin they want me to give them now, not even a
smile then. But I had the clothes. I could teach
some old biddies how to dress. Even in a tweed suit

I was striking in my fur collars, Jackie Kennedy hats.
I liked the pink satin evening gowns with gloves. Maybe
someday you'll be an airline hostess somebody said.
Well I'm a lot more than that now. A teacher, a doctor,
an astronaut even. And with my bendable legs, I'm an
amazing gymnast. I can be whatever I want to be with
my 19 inch waist and I no longer define myself by any

relationship to men. In fact, it's the other way around: think
of poor Ken, think about goofy Scotty. I never had to marry.
Even with my 39 inch bust, I don't have to nurse babies. I'm
so sexy, some have tried to ban me but the children revolted.
I'm a feminist but sometimes I do let Ken drive. I have so
many shoes– I'd rather be in sneakers – these shoes hurt.
But I smile and make myself available since so many girls
need new Barbies after their brothers, to get my attention,
cut off my head

BARBIE DREAMS OF A TORSO GIVING BIRTH

thinks at least
she has arms
and legs, long
as strands
of banyan, of
vines anyone could
twist around
their waist,
swing by. But
she feels as much
a hole, just a space
for a penis to plunge
in and some
men, seeing her
perfect, suppose
she doesn't have
a head, is a
rubber cylinder
with hair they
can stuff them
selves into like a
greased empty
toilet paper roll
what they had
used has been flushed from

Lyn Lifshin

Three from OUTRUN YOUR FATE #49

a man-sized hole

Neddy gazes into the darkness & hears
the early morning waves slapping
the shore as Joe works the shovel
into the sand-dune deeper & deeper
a man sized hole for that fucking idiot
would-be-gangster Jones who just had
to go & Neddy looks out across the bay
recalling his childhood holidays at the
beach his brother holding his head
under the water & soon the hole is dug
& Neddy & Joe push the limp body
into the grave a cold dark wind blows
across the water Neddy brushes the sand
off his jeans and says come on mate
let's go have a few beers.

the dark shadow

Neddy is dreaming the same dream he
always dreams the one where he's running
for his life down a long white corridor
& every door he opens he looks inside
& sees himself dying & in some rooms
he's hanging from the ceiling & in some
he's been shot & in others he can see
knife wounds all over his body but
the worst ones are the rooms where
he's not hurt at all yet when he stares
into his own eyes he can see the dark
shadow of death slowly entering
his shaking body & his wife says
wake up Neddy! & when Neddy comes
round the shaking has stopped
but the shadow on his eyes is still there.

outrun your fate

Neddy shadow boxes in his cell
his feet moving like Nureyev like Ali
on a good night throwing uppercuts
& jabs & hooks with horrifying power his
six-foot-three inch frame dripping with
rancid sweat in the stale afternoon air
& his cellmate Mick the Grumbler says
you can run around your cell all
you want Ned but you can't outrun
your fate & Neddy spins & throws a left
hook that stops an inch in front
of the Grumbler's face & the Grumbler
says lucky you missed asshole & Neddy
says when you got one of these you
make your own fate.

Glenn Cooper

Two from DIGGING MY OWN GRAVE AND ENJOYING THE WORK #50

not Chet

James Dean cool
before James Dean was cool
smooth trumpet
smooth voice
smooth
into the vein
junk is not a fine wine
you do not age better
older
hard lines
fallen teeth
smashed trumpet outside
Amsterdam window
listening- remembering
Tony
a junky a friend
who never played the trumpet
never was James Dean cool
loved the needle
a friend who never stayed at my place
he would rob you if he could
and rape your ass in your sleep
died
hooking for dope
a few remember him
the ones who are dead

Save Yourself, I'm Tired

Driving down the street I saw Jesus hitchhiking;
I pulled over on the side of the road.
He sat down, aren't you Jesus?
Yes, how can you tell?
The holes in your hands and feet.
Does it hurt?
No, just itches.
Where are you going?
Away.
Why?
I just want to have some fun. I'm tired of   saving people.
He looked at me. Don't even ask.
Don't worry. I'm an atheist.
I just want to be left alone, why do you think I was crucified.
I don't know, why?
The sermon gig was getting tiresome   everybody wanted something
        from me. Now, my dad wants me   to save your asses again,
        no way.
I'm going to Vegas, to drink and get laid.
You got any money?
He smirked, all the money I need.
You don't have any pockets.
I don't need pockets. I'm Jesus.
He wouldn't stop talking about his   problems. A whining Jesus
        is not what I expected.
Stop here, I'm hungry.
This place has the greatest food I'll be   back in a second.
Okay. I watched him enter McDonald's
        then I left.

Ed Jamieson Jr.

An Excerpt from THE PAINTER #51

he deepens the shadow
between the orphaned waiter,
& the wealthy spinster
with five secret abortions

murk flows into
an arcle orb

he leans forward to
whiten the brittle yearning
in the waiter's eyes

at 3 o'clock the warden
chants a psalm
to the cavalcade of literati
wandering between the spaces
of the olive trees

the muse drops in
to check
on his progress,
her inspiration
is extraneous,
yet she refuses to leave

he nods to the muse,
& lightens the pain of glasses
clinking against each other

the Sanskrit steps
& palm trees
form a pact of neutrality

the orphaned waiter stares
at the wealthy spinster -
she seems oddly familiar

Marie Lecrivain

Three from TAPPING ASHES IN THE DARK #52

Meditation on Smoking

I like the way the lighter kick starts beneath my thumb and cuts the darkness
I like the way the cherry ember glows beneath my nose leading the path to
nowhere
I like the way smoke gets pulled into the wind as I stand on the old patio
I like the way smoke hits the large bookshelf then spreads out like the tree of
no-knowledge
I like the way the smoke curls up through the lamp shades like genie-hobos
with empty pockets
I like the way I can stick my fist through the thick cloud in the tiny livingroom
I like the way the sulfur smells like the devil when I wave the wooden match
out
I like the way the smoke goes out the window like an escaped convict
I like the way the cigars wait in their box like unborn children
I like the way smoke repels a fly when I blow it at its dark wings
I like the way smoke sits in the sunrays like a decrepit gray rainbow
I like the way smoke hangs like a map of the place I came from before I was
born
I like the way the cigar cannibalizes itself as it sits in the groove of the ashtray
I like the way smoke hangs in the air justifying my laziness
I like the way smoke sits and waits, sad ether, if the windows are shut
I like the way the red hot tip shows how flimsy flesh is when I hold the cherry
against my palm
I like the way the ashes fold at the tip like a tiny animal brain
I like the way the stubs accumulate in the ashtray like tiny buckled water
pipes
I like the way the way the outer leaf unravels like a miniature nervous break-
down
I like the way smoke flows upward like a crazy maverick stream
I like the way smoke slips into the braids of the rug
I like the way smoke haunts the fibers of my shirt
I like the way smoke clouds my face in the mirror while washing my hands
I like the way smoke sit in the center of the room like a fat gray Buddha
I like the way the smoke smell comes out of my copy of Schopenhauer
I like the way smoke uncurls from my mouth like the great silent tongue of
god

belts of nails

lay down the line
sharper, harder, pal
lay down something
that resembles those
spike-strips that the police
lay out on the road
to bring a high speed chase
to its end
steal their tools
but steer clear
of the cop-soul
be the outlaw in the car
they're chasing
lay down the line, pal
belts of nails

Black Wires and Cigarettes Burns

She used to say that
my birthmarks
(I have many)
were constellations
and she'd press her
finger to each one
and try to connect them
she'd grab the dark hairs
that covered my forearms
twist and play with them
run them between her fingers
call me her wolf
but now my birthmarks are
all cigarette burns again
and my forearms are covered
with black wires again

Rob Plath

Two from BARE FEET, BROKEN GLASS (POEMS FOR ROSE) #53

what she saw there

was
one hundred eighty pounds
of pure wrath.

hair sticking out
in
crazy little clumps,
stabbing blue eyes,
slaughtering white teeth
revealed by
a rictus grin,
spittle flying
with each breath.

she saw
the stone fist
flying at
her smashed face
at speeds made
faster than light
by
uncomprehending terror.

she saw her
grandmother's
delicate blue vase
on the mantle
as she flew
across the room.

she saw him say
I love you,
woman.

she saw a little
pool of
bright, bright red
she needed to clean

as her head
hit
the otherwise
spotless floor.

what she didn't see
was
any way out.

dear buk

I, too, had a bluebird, once.

he would sing
so sweetly
as I put on my
sunday-go-to-meeting
pretty dress
on my bruised body,

as I patted makeup,
applied lipstick
to my black eyes
and busted, fat lips,
wincing when it touched
the cuts;

he would trill beautifully
when my man
held my sore hand
to tell me how much
he loved me,
how I was the only one
who ever understood,
who ever meant anything,

how sorry he was,

how it would
never happen again.

that bluebird

whipped up entire symphonies
when red roses
or
a fistful of wildflowers
(my favorites)
appeared on the kitchen table
by way of
apology

on a day when
I cried to brush my hair
in a new style
meant to hide
the scabbed bald spot.

yeah,
I had a bluebird once.

I throttled that
lying
little
bastard.

Anita Wynn

Three from THE HUNGER #54

All the Romantic Places in the World

Being part of a secret
Is a guilty pleasure
That in the beginning
Is deliciously sweet
And in the end
Is as bitter a pill to swallow
As was ever prescribed
If you're good
You get to come back
If you're not good enough
It's just one of those things
But after the blush
Wears off
After you've gotten
A few affairs under your belt
You begin to long for
What you cannot have
And when you realize
That you cannot have what
True lovers have
A sadness overtakes you
Which almost certainly
Guarantees that you will
Always be in the shadows
Giving solace and
Receiving it in kind
Behind closed doors
Whilst true lovers
Laugh and kiss and
Touch each other in all
The romantic places
In the world

This Thing In My Chest

Our passion: like
Neolithic eruption
volcanic epicenter
birthing smoldering
raw, molten energy
untamed
unconquered.

And from that union:
a portion of glass
as dark as coal
as smooth as silk
as cold as your last
off-handed remark.

Now when I think of you
I can scarcely breathe
as if the thing in my chest
would cut me with it's
razor edges.
It rests easy beneath
my sternum, a dead spot
where I let you place your
beautiful / terrible gift:
this gemstone of our passion
this flowering obsidian chunk.

You are not like
some bird of prey
(Yet there you seem to be)
perched on a stony crag
high above me waiting
for a stumble in judgment
to betray my location
to your hungry eyes.

I will pull out this
artifact of our passion
and fashion it into a dagger
black and deadly
wicked sharp
and give it back to you

I'm sure you can find some
other place to shove it.

CHOPIN

What I remember most
Is this feeling of
Holiday
Knowing that
It would end
And the drudgery
Of the world would
Soon return

So I savored the
Moments as best I could
Knowing that I was
Somewhat handicapped
By my lack of sophistication
In certain realms

We labored
Loved and
Lived within the walls
Of our respective hearts
Citadels really and
I do miss you

Miss your playing the piano most
So delicate and alive
A common thing for you
For me
The sweetest pleasure
Like a ray of light in the murkiest catacomb or
A soft hand caressing my grizzled cheek
My God
It was a sound that touched me
The clod
As deeply as possible
Making me want to climb
Mountains in your name
To worship you by
Loving you in the sweetest way
To lay at your feet
The sum total of my wealth

Your laughter
Your kisses
Chopin
This is what I miss

RD Armstrong

Three from AS IF #55

Mornings of Flowers

Friday, 8 a.m., passing through for more coffee, reaching
for the phantom cigarette, pausing at one kitchen window
then another to sight him, the man I need to believe
is always the same man who lopes up my front steps
from a dust-colored van, carrying misted flowers, slipping them
into the stoic vase, out all night, hugging the door.

He's eluded me again, but I've spotted my flowers, snuggling
in translucent, finger-painted paper and I rush, dismissing
my ignorance of any name beyond rose or daisy, to grin and coo
over this week's shapes and colors; a gift from my sister
of many years, not blood; fresh love and flowers, every

Friday morning, to help loosen the trap of terror and fatigue
from one of those life-tricks making a home in my body.

And they do. Help me. For long, luxurious moments
through these dry August dawns ... melding into September's
searing midday winds ... easing into October and mercifully
cooler nights ... November's promises ... December's distractions,
and then, finally January: glowing, glorious January, the ultimate
week of January, when scars hiding the slashes will be blending,
nicely; when the burn will have already tanned and peeled,
and the last of the poison pumps it's way out of my veins.

How I long to shake off these aromas of comfort, to shed myself
of my own uneasy excess and stand naked again; to miss
these mornings of flowers

The Knot

There's this knot in my head
left behind in all the commotion, poked at
on occasion, by makers of metaphors.   I

snatched it back, yesterday,
when no one was looking, dropped it into
a Jack & Jill bucket to soak and struggle for air

under silk, or maybe circle a sleek
swimsuit or stick itself inside stiff
panties; pretty though with burgundy lace
hugging the longest leg
right up to the ass.

*

It is my knot, after all.   I
raised it, dripping, laid it in the sun
to tighten   tough   like rope
from an 18th century ship
to confound the inattentive

to outwit the metaphors, plotting
to twist unwieldy strands of grief
into a sigh   or dull ecstasy into a smile
It's my knot   after all   the last
of my kind; dare me   promise me   a pod
or a box of native soil or Saint Theresa's

rapture.   Whose pain would I feel then?
If the loops of my knot were loosened
by strangers, whose chances would I take ?

As If

Standard advice to the diseased,
the lucky ones who function normally,
without notice.

Don't dwell, they say, don't let it
consume you, don't speculate --
live your life not what-if,
but as-if ....

Bizarre world, unfair, of course,
where, some moveable tally of moments
after the stunning numbness of words
and matching numbers deserts her,
a late-blossoming adult female, or her
senior-discount-hunting father or her 8th grader
discovers that lifetime is a crapshoot,

that gods are air and stone and like
a good game, that thumbs up - thumbs
down is whim and whim
is not deferrable;
neither is hope,
a burden of manners
immortally imposed,
a gesture
to tame madness
into constructs
of treatments, check-ups,
survival rates - something
to underline on your to-do
list and stick in your pocket,
whistling, functioning normally,
without notice, as if
you're still
like everyone else.

Angela C. Mankiewicz

Three from I SAW IT ON T.V. #56

AN ENCOUNTER WITH TOM CRUISE 11/1/07

I was on the sidewalk outside the Cinerama Dome
when Tom Cruise was talking to paparazzi
about his latest movie LIONS FOR LAMBS.

Feeling a bit irreverent, I yelled to Tom,
HOW DOES IT FEEL BEING FORTY-FIVE?

Silence.

Then Tom said:
I'm not forty-five.
I'm thirty-five.
Next year, I'll be thirty-four.
How old are you?

I hesitated to answer.
But a few seconds of intense, irritated stares
from members of the Entertainment Media
changed my mind.

I said:
I'm forty-eight.
Next year, I'll be forty-nine.

Tom said:
Thanks so much
for explaining the difference
between you and me.

The Entertainment Media applauded
as I left the scene of my verbal crime
and headed to Amoeba Records
to track down VHS/DVD copies
of THE PICTURE OF DORIAN GRAY.

MITT ROMNEY'S LAP DANCE

Go to a tiny dressing room.

Put on an American flag bikini,
using falsies borrowed from Rudy Giuliani's
dress-in-drag-for-laughs wardrobe.

Make sure your Mormon underwear
stays firmly underneath your bikini briefs.

Wait for George Herbert Walker Bush
to knock on the dressing room door.

Walk with Bush 41 to the back room
where Bible-believing Fundamentalist Christians await.

Choose a Fundamentalist Christian.

Ask him to sit in a chair.

Whisper into his ear:
Yes, I believe the entire Bible should be taken literally.
Elect me and I'll do anything you want.

Go into your dance.

Start slowly as the jukebox plays
Lee Greenwood's GOD BLESS THE USA.

Then get more excited and feverish as
the music switches to Contemporary Christian goddesses
such as Jaci Velasquez and pre-1985 Amy Grant.

Get close to the Fundamentalist Christian
without touching him.

Excite him again and again
until he yells HALLELUJAH!
and stuffs a roll of thousand-dollar bills
between your bikini briefs and Mormon underwear.

Let Bush 41 lead you out of the room.

Listen to him as he croaks:
You gotta keep turning these people on

Then hold them at arm's length.
Who cares if they whine?
They have no place to go.
But you saw something that Bush 41 didn't:
the Fundamentalist Christian's hunger
for someone to deliver on his desire
for the United States to re-adopt values
cherished long ago—in Salem, Massachusetts.

You might want to be nothing more
than the CEO of the United States,
continuing the erosion of the government
in favor of more privatization and profiteering.

But the Fundamentalist Christian
wants you to do God's Will.

And God help you
if you're in the White House
on January 20, 2009
and you fail to return his calls.

SHALLOW AL

It's déjà vu again in the year 2008.

Remember two years previous
when living-in-comfort progressives
were all agog to Al Gore's environmental documentary
AN INCONVENIENT TRUTH
which was a boring PowerPoint show
about an admittedly serious problem called global warming
climaxed by Melissa Etheridge righteously braying
a song called "I Want to Wake Up"?

Remember one year previous
when lots of people sat by the TV and radio
to hear favorite musical acts take part
in Al Gore's LIVE EARTH?

Maybe I'd join the cheerleading if Al Gore

would do a better job of holding corporations responsible
for the amount of pollution they contribute
and the balking they tend to do at establishing standards
for cleaning up their acts
(let's shoot for a target date of.....2024).
Instead, it's just a bunch of platitudes
along the lines of:
Here, little people,
change your light bulbs,
use your air conditioners less,
shower within 90 seconds and
buy hybrid cars.

All well and good,
but it's not enough
until the corporations—the Big People—
try harder to go Green,
even if it's out of nothing more noble
than saving money.

Two nights ago,
I saw Al Gore on 60 MINUTES
with Lesley Stahl looking like
she wanted to sit on his lap.

And I noticed the expensive TV ad campaign
with cutely-matched opposites
(Al Sharpton and Pat Robertson, anyone?)
to get people to save energy.

And I wondered how much of a carbon footprint
was created to make this orgy of self-congratulation happen.

Terry McCarty

Three from WHIPPED CREAM AND SUSHI #57

felony assault with a deadly weapon

not a firearm
but a handy empty wine bottle
his blood
much brighter than
the cabernet sauvignon
it had contained

i've been busy
nursing welts from
plastic handcuffs

don't mess with me you
fucked up meth bitch!
i'm in here for
felony assault with a deadly weapon!

wrap your arms around your head
when you sleep

jail? i've seen it before
& it's becoming a bore

not exactly the belly of the beast
as i cry quietly
inside
'but i'm the victim'

i'm my own victim of
my own shortcomings
& sins
they close the metal doors

i wrap my arms
around my own head
& try to sleep on concrete floors
colder than my heart.

what makes their eyes go dead

you always hear how their eyes
were black holes
as they committed some
atrocity
like the man
who just stomped his
2 year old to death
killing him way past dead
last weekend in california
or the woman who
drove a knife repeatedly into
her aging father's back
or even my cousin
as he held his young wife's
shot gurgling body down
so it could bleed out
while family and cops
stood in horror
and we saw black holes
dead eyes in his face
he didn't even look like my cousin
some zombie stranger instead
just like the father killing his
baby son
people holler
people grab at them
they don't hear
their black eyes don't see
they just do what they do
as if possessed

where is the chemistry in this?
somebody tell me
there is an explanation
and don't tell me about the devil
tell me how
the 'normal' person
suddenly does these things?
the good neighbor
the good co-worker
the good child
don't tell me about the devil
but i do believe
their soul is gone

how did that happen?
what ate it up?
and can we make it stop doing that?

whipped cream and sushi

we planned a picnic
alongside the river
but the skies darkened
and the winds blew
instead we
spread the blanket on the floor
and opened the curtains wide
he brought the sushi
i brought the whipped cream.

nila northSun

Three from THE MYSTERIOUS WOMAN NEXT DOOR #58

How It Started

Three black nickels
and a rusty quarter,
she said it was a sign,
told you to keep them
hidden –
that it could
mean something.
You add a bent dime,
bought a paper,
shuffled through to your
horoscope.
All it said was,
"You should
have listened."

The Space Between Breaths

Reading her poem
I notice
the difference between
the words –
"lovelies"
and "love lies" –
is only
one small gap,
a pause,
no more
than the space
between
breaths...

Somebody

There's that day,
that one day,
that you're the best
you're ever going to be.

For some it comes early,
then you spend the rest of your days
on that long slide
to the bottom.

For others, it comes late.
You've clawed your way
to the top.
They look at you
like you're somebody.
You never want to let go.
You know,
you'd tear the hearts out of the angels
to make it last
just a little longer.

For the rest of us,
there isn't much.
When it comes,
it's no-big-deal.
The grocery clerk
still doesn't stop,
turn her head and say,
"Hey man,
you're looking sharp."
And the gal at the bank,
the teller,
forgets your name
for the hundredth time.
And if the guy
from the power company
is coming to turn you off,
it'll be late on a Friday,
to late
to make a call.
They'd leave you
shivering in the dark,
till Monday.
It's not
that you're a loser,
it's just that,
they never let you win.
Not even
on that day,
that one day
when you're the best
you're ever going to be.

W. S. Gainer

Two from HESITANT COMMITMENTS #59

Postcards from your hideaway in Scotland

You write that I'm a bird, hungry
for the wind, alive in my mouth, the sun
scrolling my shoulders, come daybreak.
You want me to nest, be your hearth, warming
you, my heartbeat to be your tambourine
jangling along the impatient hills and moors.
You wish my voice to soothe the ravens
that stretch mourning bands around your cottage
during this isolation from each other.
I send you notes on cast-away
newspapers, the backs of torn photos,
once, on the side of a fallen leaf.
I mail feathers, freshly picked flowers,
a shell shaped like a bugle.
This is me, I tell you.
This is who I am.

Redemption

You lower me into the quivering Mediterranean,
your arms incandescent under the burn of the rising moon.
I become the Swan Princess, drawn back
from my feathered fate, Ophelia,
resuscitated before the drowning was complete,
Ann Frank, rescued from that attic
before the Nazi's promises became as lifeless bodies
along the littered streets.
We lie on the beach after,
watch the sand glitter on bare skin,
lost gods, finding our way home.
You reach over and take my hand.
A dark bird of sorrow rises finally from my chest,
flaps into the indecipherable night.

Pris Campbell

Three from THE WREN NOTEBOOK
LRBMS* #1

The wind is a street gang
on the west end of Dakota.
It blows us so hard, we
cannot recover. It blows us
flat, blows us
like darts sideways
into barns, south, if we're lucky
but then, we need permission
to leave. We are expelled
yet we are charged with
abandonment. We are
at large.
There is no easy passage
on the west end of Dakota.

It's about heat and rhythm
this little heart pounding
to the limit an alarm
clock at the crack of dawn.
Wren does not fly that straight
but this time
it's a bee line close
enough to straight.
There is really no need for straight lines.
It's about heat and rhythm.

A splash of orange
slanders a black sky
and the wren heads for cover.
The wren is a recurrent figure.
She has a beak
and she can crack small things.
She has an eye

for lateral moments.
There are facts
that blur the line
between
the garden and the natural world.
And there are crows. They
lift off from limbs
in the orange grove out back
and under cover of that sweet air
they land like WWII bombers
inside the garden.
Inside we wait for hunger.
Outside we wait for movement.
We want what is inside to go away.
We want what is outside
to be prey. On this morning,
fortune is with us.
The crows won't even play
on this turf.
There is big work
in other parts.
And wren
has a throat
reserved for cricket
and song.
It is cricket and song
that lead her
under moonlight
over stone.

Rick Smith

°LRBMS is a series of books that never quite got off the ground, Rick's book being the only one to date to be published.

Bios

RD Armstrong, aka Raindog, has been at this since the early nineties. He has self-published, through his Lummox Press, 17 books. He's also had books published by 12 Gauge Press and Vinegar Hill Books. In addition to his own work, the Lummox Press has published over 60 titles by poets, both known and unknown covering the broad spectrum of Small Press poetry. He published a monthly magazine, The Lummox Journal, for over ten years (it's now online). Recent titles include Fire and Rain – Selected Poems 1992-2007 Vol. 1 & 2, On/Off the Beaten path – The road Poems, and El Pagano and Other Twisted Tales (short stories). www.lummoxpress.com

Pris Campbell's poetry has appeared in Poems Niederngasse, Boxcar Poetry Review, MiPo (digital/print/radio/OCHO), Thunder Sandwich, MEAT, The Dead Mule, Empowerment4Women, In The Fray, The Cliffs: Soundings, Dufus, and The Wild Goose Review. She has three chaps: Abrasions (Rank Stranger Press), Interchangeable Goddesses (Rose of Sharon/3 Virgins) and Hesitant Commitments (Lummox Press). A former Clinical Psychologist, she's now sidelined by CFIDS. She lives in the greater West Palm Beach, FL , with her husband. More of her poetry can be found at her website (http://www.poeticinspire.com) and her MySpace blog (http://www.myspace.com/priscampbell)

Alan Catlin has recently retired from 34 years of working in his unchosen profession as barman to work on his fictional memoirs. He recently finished a novel about his working years called Chaos Management and is putting together a related book of stories to be called Hours of Happiness. His next scheduled chapbook of poetry is Only the dead Know Albany forthcoming from Sunnyoutside Press.

Patricia Cherin coordinates the Humanities Master of Arts External degree (HUX) program at Cal State University Dominguez Hills. She has over 100 publications and lives in Long Beach at the edge of the continent.

Leonard J. Cirino b. 1943. Author of over twenty-five chapbooks and collections of poems from various presses in the past twentyone years. He lives in Springfield, Oregon, and has devoted over three decades to reading, writing, editing, and publishing poetry. His book THE TERRIBLE WILDERNESS OF SELF was nominated for the National Book Award in poetry, 1998. Recent chapbooks include, The Widow Poems, (Lone Willow Press – 2001).

Glenn W. Cooper lives and writes in Tamworth, Australia. He works as an inventory manager in a independent bookstore. His latest chapbooks are

'Some Natural Things' via Kamini Press, and 'Rimbaud In The City: 10 Snapshots" from Kendra Steiner Editions. He can be contacted via his My Space page at http://www.myspace.com/muhhamadaali.

Hugh Fox is originally from Chicago (b.1932). For years Fox edited the poetry mag Ghost Dance. He was intimately involved with COSMEP--The Committee of Small Magazine Editors and publishers, has 105 books published, the latest The Collected Poetry (540 pp., from World Audience), and poetry chapbooks Alex (Rubicon Press), Ghosts (Green Panda Press) and La Paix/Peace (Higganum Hill Press).

Bill Gainer is known for the openness of his confessional poetry and is recognized as one of the founding contributors to the modern movement of "After Hours" poetry. Gainer has contributed to the literary scene as a writer, editor, promoter, publicist and poet. He is a co-founder and current board member of the Nevada County Poetry Series. Gainer has read and worked with a wide range of poets and writers, including readings on KUSF with Punk-Rocker Patti Smith and performing with California's Poet Laureate, Al Young. Gainer is nationally published and continues to be a sought after reader, he can be previewed on **youtube.com – search Bill Gainer**

Mark Hartenbach's latest book is The Sound of from Hcolom Press. his latest chapbooks from Pudding House Press are Three Poems & Surfing The Infinite Pulse.

Scott Holstad has authored 15 published collections of poetry since 1991. His work has appeared in hundreds of magazines in 26 countries and five languages, including The Minnesota Review, Wisconsin Review, Hawaii Review, Pacific Review, Exquisite Corpse, Caffeine, Chiron Review, Lullwater Review, Poetry Ireland Review, Arkansas Review, Asheville Poetry Review, and Southern Review.

Larry Jaffe has been, for his entire professional career, using his art to promote human rights. He was the poet-in-residence at the Autry Museum of Western Heritage, a featured poet in Chrysler's Spirit in the Words poetry program, co-founder of Poets for Peace (now Poets for Human Rights) and helped spearhead the United Nations Dialogue among Civilizations through Poetry project which incorporated hundreds of readings in hundreds of cities globally using the aesthetic power of poetry to bring understanding to the world. To reward this commitment was recently appointed Poet Laureate for Youth for Human Rights. He was the recent recipient of the Saint Hill Art Festival's Lifetime of Creativity Award, the first time given to a poet. www.youthforhumanrights.org

Edward Jamieson, Jr. has a wife and two kids and works at a government job. He lives and writes and does other stuff in Southern California, south of

Disneyland. He has been published in various rags and has been honored to be the poetry editor for Lummox Journal. His latest chapbook is Digging My Grave and Enjoying the Work.

Patricia Wellingham-Jones has written Don't Turn Away: Poems About Breast Cancer and End-Cycle: Poems about caregiving, among others. She is a three-time Pushcart Prize nominee and her work is published in numerous anthologies, journals and Internet magazines. A cancer survivor, she has a longtime interest in 'healing writing' and the benefits people gain from writing and reading their work together. Her website is www.wellinghamjones.com

Jacqueline Kras is an artist living somewhere in Lost Angeles.

Marie Lecrivain is the editor of poeticdiversity: the litzine of Los Angeles. She's been published in a number of journals, including 400 words, Subtle Tea, and Earth's Daughters; dabbles in digital photography, and occasionally plays well with others…

Frances LeMoine has dropped off the grid. She used to publish the fine magazine Flash!Point.

Linda Lerner is the author of twelve poetry collections, the most recent being Living in Dangerous Times (Pressa Press – 2007); & City Woman (March Street Press - 2006); (both were Small press Picks); Because You Can't I Will (Pudding House - 2005). March Street Press published The Bowery And Other Poems which was a Small Press Review pick of the month. She has been twice nominated for a pushcart prize. In 1995 she and Andrew Gettler began Poets on the line, (http://www.echonyc.com/~poets) the first poetry anthology on the Net. Her poems have / will recently appeared in Tribes, Onthebus, The Paterson Literary Review, The New York Quarterly, Home Planet News, The Lummox Journal and Van Gogh's Ear.
http://www.nyqpoets.net/poet/lindalerner

Philomene Long, b. 1940 – d. 2007. Former nun and Venice beach poet, dubbed "Queen of Bohemia" by her compatriots, Philomene was an internationally published poet and film director. Her books include The Book of Sleep, The Ghosts of Venice West with John Thomas. Her most recent books (beside her LRBs) were Bukowski in the Bathtub and American Zen Bones. Her films include The Beats: An Existential Comedy with Allen Ginsberg.

Lyn Lifshin is one of the most prolific and widely published poets in America. Her books include Another Woman Who Looks Like Me (selected for the 2007 Paterson Award for Literary Excellence for previous finalists of the Paterson Poetry Prize); The Licorice Daughter: My Year With Ruffian; Before it's Light; Cold Comfort. Pending publication are: Barbaro, Beyond Brokenness; Persephone; and Lost In The Fog. Her poems have appeared in most literary and poetry magazines and she is the subject of an award winning documentary film, Lyn Lifshin: Not Made of Glass, available from Women Make Movies. For interviews, photographs, more bio material, samples of work and more, her web site is www.lynlifshin.com

Gerald Locklin is now a Lecturer in the Master of Professional Writing Program at the University of Southern California and a Professor Emeritus of English at California State University, Long Beach, where he taught from 1965 through 2007. He is the author of over 125 books, chapbooks, and broadsides of poetry, fiction, and criticism, with over 3000 poems, stories, articles, reviews, and interviews published in periodicals. His most recent books and chapbooks include Gerald Locklin: New and Selected Poems, and The Cezanne/Pissarro Poems, both from World Parade Books. A website and occasional blog are in progress at www.geraldlocklin.com.

Laura Joy Lustig is a fine arts photographer in NYC. It is rumored that she has wisely moved on from poetry.

Angela Consolo Manckiewicz has 4 chapbooks out, the most recent are AN EYE (Pecan Grove Press - 2006) and AS IF (Lummox Press - 2008),. Prizes include a Grand Prize sestina from TRELLIS, a 2nd prize poem from Jersey-Works, 1st-prize broadside from AMELIA, Pushcart nomination from Hammers, and a Writers Digest Honorable Mention for my play, JUDGMENTS. Publications include: PRESA, Montserrat, Re)Verb, Sketchbook, Seldom Nocturne, Arsenic Lobster, Temple/Tsunami, Butcher Block, Slipstream, Chiron Review, Hawaii Review, Cerberus, Karamu, Lynx Eye, Pemmican, Blind Man's Rainbow and ArtWord. Her children's stories, THE GRUMMEL BOOK, are being reissued on CD in 2008 by SHOOFLY. www.POETACMANK.blogspot.com

Terry McCarty has been a part of the Southern California poetry scene since 1998. His chapbooks include HOLLYWOOD POETRY, 20 GREATEST HITS VOLUMES 1 AND 2 and WICHITA FALLS. Terry's poem "Icarus' Itinerary" appears in the Tebot Bach anthology SO LUMINOUS THE WILDFLOWERS.

Rebecca Morrison has published several chapbooks including Raining All Over (2003); Matsuyoi: 50 Haiku for the Moon (2000); The Cook Inlet Poems (2005); Border Crossing (2006); A Celtic Epic (2007); and Two Hundred Ridge Haiku for Lew Welch (2008). She has worked for 30 years at UC Davis where she graduated summa cum laude in 1992. She has published interviews, editorials, short stories, photos, essays and articles and she has been interviewed by the Sacramento Bee, the Sacramento News and Review, the Davis Enterprise, and the University of California Davis Cal Aggie. She is editor and creator of eskimopie.net which has run for 6 years. She is the co-founder of the Third Sunday Writing Group which has met monthly for

13 years. She recently edited and published a poetry anthology for the Towe Auto Museum.

Todd Moore is the co founder of the Outlaw Poetry Movement, along with Tony Moffeit. His latest books in the ongoing Dillinger saga include RELENTLESS and TELL THE CORPSE A STORY, both from Crane's Bill Press. His work also appears in THE OUTLAW BIBLE OF AMERICAN POETRY. Todd and his son Theron co edit the online zine St. Vitus which can be viewed at www.saintvituspress.com

B.Z. Niditch is a poet, playwright, fiction writer and teacher, as well as the founder and artistic director of Boston's THE ORIGINAL THEATRE. His work is widely published in journals and magazines throughout the world, including: Columbia: A Magazine of Poetry and Art; The Literary Review; Denver Quarterly; Hawaii Review; Le Guepard (France); Kadmos (France); Prism International; Jejune (Czech Republic); Leopold Bloom (Budapest); Antioch Review; and Prairie Schooner, among others. He lives in Brookline, Massachusetts.

Normal is a wailer and eccentric late-night howler. He lives near Woodstock in the Hudson River Valley. He can trace his poetic roots back to the early 60s where he cut his teeth on the WORD in New York's East Village.

nila northSun has served on the Nevada State Arts Council from 2000-2001, and on the Nevada Women's Commission in 1992. After participating in the Taos Poetry Circus in 1997, she began hosting the first poetry slams in Reno in the late 90's. Her achievements in literature include the Silver Pen award in 2000, the Indigenous Heritage award in 2004, and her books include: Diet Pepsi, Nacho Cheese; Coffee, Dustdevils, And Old Rodeo Bulls; Little Bones, Small Eyes, A Snake In Her Mouth; and Love At Gunpoint. nilanorthsun. blogspot.com and www.myspace.com/nilanorthsun

Rob Plath is a 38 year old poet from New York. Raised in Brooklyn, and a former student of Allen Ginsberg, Rob has published 5 chapbooks of poetry. He is proud to have Raindog's Lummox Press be the publisher of his latest one.

Bill Shields was published by 2.13.61 Press and gained some notoriety as a writer about Vietnam & PTSD. He enjoyed some success as a poet, was widely published and has since gone off the grid.

Rick Smith is a clinical psychologist who specializes in domestic violence and brain damage; he practices in Rancho Cucamonga, CA. He is also a blues harmonica player with many recording credits. Check out www.mescalsheiks. com for a sample of his recent music. Look for new poems in Onthebus, Blueline, Hanging Loose, Lalitamba, Paper Street and Rattle.

Belinda Subraman lives in Ruidoso, New Mexico. Her poetry has appeared in Puerto del Sol, Main Street Rag, Big Bridge ,Babel Fruit, mgversion2, Electica, Social Justice and Unlikely Stories to name a few. Since 2005 she has been interviewing poets, musicians and activists on her weekly radio show and podcast called Belinda Subraman Presents / The Gypsy Art Show http://belinda_subraman.podomatic.com . For ten years she was editor and publisher of Gypsy Literary Magazine and Vergin' Press. Her main web site is http://belindasubraman.com

John Sweet, b. 1968. Devourer of souls, impaler of the oppressors, dedicated civil servant; opposed to all schools of poetry & organized religions. Collections of peace & tranquility include HUMAN CATHEDRALS, FALSE HOPE and ENEMY.

Will Taylor, Jr. lives in San Francisco with his wife and a cat named Trouble. His work has been widely published in the independent press and across the internet in such publications as Poesy, Anthills and The Chiron Review. His work is scheduled to appear in upcoming issues of the New York Quarterly and his latest book, Words For Songs Never Written, a selection of new and collected poems, is now available from Centennial Press. A book of new work is currently in progress with Sunnyoutside Press. Visit him at http://www.williamtaylorjr.com

John Thomas, b.1930 – d. 2002. In 1959, during the Beat era, John rode his thumb from Baltimore to the West Coast (San Francisco and Venice, CA), where he lived and wrote until his untimely death at the age of 71.His books include John Thomas, Epopocia and the Decay of Satire, Cinq, Abandoned Latitudes, Old Man Stravinsky Rehearses with Orchestra, Nevertheless – and (with his life partner poet Philomene Long) The Book of Sleep, The Ghosts of Venice West, and Bukowski in the Bathtub. Feeding the Animal was the last published collection of his work.

Scott Wannberg still reveres Strother Martin. Can be heard and seen on 3 Fools For April with Viggo and Henry Mortenensen, which is available from Percival Press. Voted for Barack Obama. Working on losing weight. Still writes to music and songwriters. Still not sure where it all comes from, but is happy when it shows up. He now lives in Oregon where the air is sweet.

Mark Weber lives and works in Albuquerque, NM. He is the proprietor of Zerx Books & Recordings and has a show on the radio. He has published numerous chapbooks with Gerald Locklin and has an amazing library of recordings (both music and spoken word) which he has been working on for many, many years.

Lawrence Welsh's sixth book of poetry, SKULL HIGHWAY, was published in 2008 by La Alameda Press. A chapbook, DEL REY RACA, is forthcoming from The Silver Wonder Press. During the past 16 years, his work has appeared in about 200 national and regional magazines, including Puerto del Sol, Hawaii Review, Louisiana Review, Rio Grande Review, The Texas Observer, Nexus and The Wormwood Review.

Harry R. Wilkens was born in 1945 in the French/American garrison town of Kaiserslautern (in the former French Occupation Zone of Germany), nicknamed "K-Town" by the American GIs. He has been living since 1991 in Geneva and continues to write his poetry for many zines all over the world and several chapbooks, such as The Hit Man (also in Arabic), Terre Promise, Zombies (bilingual), Pig's Hell, Un autre monde, Abyss (English/Greek) and the first three versions of Piss Talks (one of them in English/Korean). In 1997, along with others, he founded the Docker Movement for free, non-adademic poetry accessible to everybody and was the editor of the Dockernet newsletter. Presently he is the columnist of the South-Korean website **www.artforumasia.com** where his musings are regulary illustrated by his friend Norman J. Olson.

Lindsay Wilson's fourth chapbook, from her red deck, was published by Pathwise Press, and his poetry and reviews have appeared in Talking River, The Small Press Review, Diner, Gulf Stream, The South Dakota Review, among others. He teaches English at Truckee Meadows Community College and edits the college's literary magazine, the Meadow, which can be viewed at **www.tmcc.edu/meadow.**

A.D. Winan's poetry, prose and photography have appeared internationally in numerous literary magazines and anthologies, including American Poetry Review (article on Bob Kaufman), Rattle, Confrontation, Poetry Now, City Lights Journal, Poetry Australia, the New York Quarterly, and the Outlaw Bible of American Poetry. In 2004 a song poem of his was performed at Tully Hall. In 2006 he was awarded a PEN Josephine Miles award for literary excellence. In 2007 Presa Press published a book of his selected poems. Sound Street Tracks will soon be releasing a new CD of his, as part of a six CD collector set. His web site: adwinans.mysite.com His blog: **myspace. com/adwinans**

Anita L. Wynn, aka Wolfie, is the author of three volumes of poetry, Speaking in Tongues, White Horses, and Bare Feet, Broken Glass...which deals with the subject of Domestic Violence. **www.myspace.com/anitawynn**

Some Comments about the Little Red Books:

"The Little Red Books are a sturdy series."—*John Berbrich*

"The presence of Lummox Press in San Pedro adds luster to the southern California literary scene, though Armstrong [editor/publisher], non-parochial, publishes a spectrum of writers from New York City westward. Other writers include Bill Shields, Laura Joy Lustig, Scott C. Holstad, normal, and William Taylor, Jr." —*Robert Peters*

Bombed in New Mexico – A collection of poetry well worth reading. The Todd Moore half will pulverize something – if not your jaw, maybe your mind. Weber's wacky imagination will keep you turning his pages. #26 in Lummox's sturdy Little Red Book series. —*John Berbrich*

Lost Highway – A blues poetry anthology, including work by Winans, John Macker, Errol Miller, and editor RD Armstrong, plus others. Filled w/lonely dirt roads, bottles of bourbon, songs, harps, & gee-tar. If you love the blues, you'll want this book. If you love poetry, you'll want this book. Simple as that. —*John Berbrich*

Rick Smith's poetry [The Wren Notebook] is eloquent, lyrical, and highly evocative of the sense of nature that us wingless creatures don't normally have access to (or have lost touch with), addressing the reader with a flutter of wings, a flash of thought, or a swoop through boundless skies. Judith Bever's pen and ink drawings compliment the poems in a thoughtful way, amplifying the already unified feeling of this collection. If the Lummox Press can maintain the standard set by this first book in their new series, then we can count on seeing more fine publications in the future. —*Mark Terrill*

Smith is a poet secure in his ability to write accessible poems that speak serious truths to the heart. This book is a pleasure to read, and one you will return to again and again. Ultimately, the desires of the wren are universal: we are all seeking contentment in a turbulent world. —*Laura Stamps*

"[On/Off the Beaten Path] is a wonderful companion volume to A Journey up the Coast illustrating this poet's agile descriptive and narrative powers."
—*Tim Scannell*

"Two friends of mine took this book [Feeding the Animal] backpacking with them and told me it was the greatest book they've read in a long time!"
—*Marsha Gertzler*

Paper Heart -- "*Real love poems. Not stupid or sentimental a bit, but rather a true portrayal of the fluttering heart in its moments of despair & ecstasy.*"
—*John Berbrich*

Feeding The Animal – "*The poems in this collection, come straight out of the spiritual essentials of life. They nurture. John Thomas is one of our best poets.*" —*John Bennett*

Late Night on the Psych Ward – "*Belinda writes factually; doesn't negate, romanticize, or over-play sentimentality about the lives of the people in her care.*" —*Joyce Metzger*

Familiarities – "*Patricia Cherin's call to "Familiarities" is a close family connection, something we all need in this day, and time; a comfort zone to call our own. Gerald Locklin's poems are centered around imprinted motifs, students, writer's woes, his love of jazz, historical facts, readers, time and western man.*"
—*Joyce Metzger*

"*Equal Opportunity SledgeHammer celebrates the yes-ness of the moment, whatever the despair of the times..*" —*G. Murray Thomas*

"*Bill Shields' Meat Eater... as concentrated and powerful as a shot glass of bleach.*" —*Rod Sperry*

THE QUEEN OF BOHEMIA and COLD EYE BURNING AT 3 A.M. – *Lummox Press has done something fine and unusual here, simultaneously publishing a "matched set" of books. Two strings, as it were, to her marvelous bow. I can hold these two little books between my palms and only their corners are visible. Such magical power in so small a space! Read them. —John Thomas*

The Official THE LITTLE RED BOOKS List°

Fool's Paradise RD Armstrong •1
El Pagano RD Armstrong •2
Equal Opportunity Sledgehammer Scott Wannberg •3
Bone Todd Moore & RD Armstrong •4
Meat Eater Bill Shields •5
Scar Tissue A.D. Winans •6
Apology to the Idiots Laura Joy Lustig •7
Eyes Like Mingus Jazz Poetry Anthology •8
Remembering Bukowski A.D. Winans •9
Journey Up The Coast RD Armstrong •10
The Lummox Sampler Various selections •11
The Inside-Out World of BZ Niditch •12
Hang Gliding On X Scott C. Holstad •13
Any Abyss Will Do William Taylor Jr. •14
Blood on the Floor normal •15
Maytag Heights Various contributors •16
ME Hugh/Connie Fox •17
The Iceberg Theory Gerald Locklin •18
No Earthly Sense Gets It Right L. Lerner •19
The Corpse Is Dreaming Todd Moore •20
Bourbon Skin Jacqueline Kras & Frances LeMoine •21
Paper Heart V. 3 Raindog •22
Blue Collar Work Errol Miller •23
Apollo's Motorcycle Frank Lonabaugh •24
Nomads of Oblivion Scott Wannberg •25
Bombed in New Mexico T. Moore - M. Weber •26
On/Off the Beaten Path RD Armstrong •27
Lost Highway Blues Poetry Anthology •28
Book of Daze Calendar with maxims by BZ Niditch •29
Cajun Flavored Mayonaise Rene Diedrich •30
Feeding the Animal John Thomas •31
LRB of Maxims BZ Niditch •32
Familiarities P. Cherin & G. Locklin •33
The Queen of Bohemia Philomene Long •34
Cold Eye Burning at 3 A.M. P. Long •35
New Shouts at Broken Dreams L. Welsh •36
Late Night in the Psych Ward B. Subraman •37
bakersfield 99 Lindsay Wilson •38
Piss Talks Harry Wilkens •39
Death & Transfiguration Cocktail A. Catlin •40
Poems of Li Xi Leonard J. Cirino •41

Paper Heart V. 4 Raindog •42
A Gathering Glance P. Wellingham-jones •43
Raining All Over Rebecca Morrison •44
American Child normal •45
L. A. Rhapsody Larry Jaffe •46
The Barbie Poems Vol. 1 Lyn Lifshin •47
The Barbie Poems Vol. 2 Lyn Lifshin •48
Outrun Your Fate Glenn Cooper •49
Digging My Own Grave Ed Jamieson Jr. •50
The Painter Marie Lecrivain •51
Tapping Ashes in the Dark Rob Plath •52
Bare Feet, Broken Glass Anita Wynn •53
The Hunger RD Armstrong •54
As If Angela C. Mankiewicz •55
I Saw it on TV Terry McCarty •56
Whipped Cream & Sushi nila northSun •57
Mysterious Woman Next Door W.S. Gainer •58
Hesitant Commitments Pris Campbell •59

Little Red Book Master Series°°

The Wren Notebook Rick Smith •1

°All LRBs are $6 (ppd – USA) , $8 (ppd - World)
°° Master Series $13 (ppd – USA), $15 (ppd - World)